MY PET RECIPES, TRIED AND TRUE

MY PET RECIPES, TRIED AND TRUE

VARIOUS

ISBN: 978-93-5344-576-8

First Published: 1900

LECTOR HOUSE LLP
E-MAIL: lectorpublishing@gmail.com

MY PET RECIPES TRIED AND TRUE

CONTRIBUTED BY THE LADIES AND FRIENDS OF ST. ANDREW'S CHURCH QUEBEC

"We may live without poetry, music and art;
We may live without conscience, and live without heart;
We may live without friends; we may live without books;
But civilized man cannot live without cooks."

—OWEN MEREDITH.

1900

RHYMES TO REMEMBER...

"Always have lobster sauce with salmon,
And put mint sauce your roasted lamb on.
In dressing salad mind this law
With two hard yolks use one raw.
Roast pork, sans apple sauce, past doubt
Is Hamlet with the Prince left out.
Broil lightly your beefsteak—to fry it
Argues contempt of christian diet.
It gives true epicures the vapors
To see boiled mutton minus capers.
Boiled turkey, gourmands know, of course
Is exquisite with celery sauce.
Roasted in paste, a haunch of mutton
Might make ascetics play the glutton.
To roast spring chickens is to spoil them,
Just split them down the back and broil them,
Shad, stuffed and baked is most delicious,
T'would have electrified Apicius.
Roast veal with rich stock gravy serve,
And pickled mushrooms too, observe,
The cook deserves a hearty cuffing
Who serves roast fowl with tasteless stuffing.
But one might rhyme for weeks this way,
And still have lots of things to say;
And so I'll close, for reader mine,
This is about the hour to dine."

CONTENTS

CONTENTS

vii

SOUP.

"The best soups are made with a blending of many flavors. Don't be afraid of experimenting with them. Where you make one mistake you will be surprised to find the number of successful varieties you can produce. If you like a spicy flavor try two or three cloves, or allspice, or bay leaves. All soups are improved by a dash of onion, unless it is the white soups, or purées from chicken, veal, fish, etc. In these celery may be used. In nothing as well as soups can a housekeeper be economical of the odds and ends of food left from meals. One of the best cooks was in the habit of saving everything, and announced one day, when her soup was especially praised, that it contained the crumbs of gingerbread from her cake box! Creamed onions left from a dinner, or a little stewed corn, potatoes mashed, a few baked beans — even a small dish of apple sauce have often added to the flavor of soup. Of course, all good meat gravies, or bones from roast or boiled meats, can be added to your stock pot. A little butter is always needed in tomato soup. In making stock, use a quart of water for every pound of meat and bone. Cut the meat in pieces, crack the bones, place all in the kettle, pour over it the proper quantity of cold water; let it soak a while on the back of the range before cooking. Let soup boil slowly, never hard, (an hour for each pound of meat) strain through a sieve or coarse cloth. Never let the fat remain on your soup. Let get cold and lift it off, or skim it off hot."

BROWN STOCK.
MRS. W. COOK.

Four pounds shin of beef, or other meats and bones — four carrots, four onions, one turnip, one small head of celery, one half tablespoonful of salt, one half teaspoonful of peppercorns, six cloves, five pints of cold water. Cut up the meat bone and place it in a large saucepan, pour over the water, skim when boiling, prepare the vegetables, add them to the saucepan; cover closely and boil slowly four hours. The spice should be added with the vegetables.

CREAM OF CELERY SOUP.
MRS. ERNEST F. WURTELE.

One quart chicken or veal broth; one quart milk; one half cupful rice; one teaspoonful salt; one head celery; seasoning. Use for this soup a quart of chicken or veal broth and about a quart of milk; pick over and wash the rice, rinse it well in cold water, and put it in a thick saucepan over the fire with a pint of milk and a teaspoonful of salt; wash a head of celery and grate the white stalks, letting the grated celery fall into milk enough to cover it; put the grated celery with the rice and gently simmer them together until the rice is tender enough to rub through a sieve with a potato masher, adding more milk if the rice absorbs what has first been put with it. After the rice has been rubbed through the sieve, return it to the saucepan, place it again over the fire, and gradually stir with it the quart of stock or broth; if this quantity of stock does not dilute the soup to a creamy consistency, add a little milk; let the soup get scalding hot, season it with salt, white pepper, and a very little grated nutmeg, and serve at once.

CELERY SOUP.
MRS. STOCKING.

Four large potatoes, three large onions, six or eight stalks of celery. Chop all the vegetables very fine, and place in an earthern kettle and cover with boiling water, stir often till cooked, then add one quart of milk and let boil; add butter, pepper and salt to taste. This receipt will serve six persons.

CHICKEN CREAM SOUP.
MRS. DUNCAN LAURIE.

Take the carcase of a roast chicken or turkey, break the bones, and cover with a quart of cold water and simmer for two hours adding boiling water, to keep the original quantity. Strain and return to kettle, add one chopped onion, two grated raw potatoes, one half small turnip grated, and one half cup rice. Boil until rice is very soft. Strain again, and return to kettle and let boil, and add one pint milk, one teaspoon cornstarch rubbed smooth in a tablespoon butter and a little salt and pepper, serve hot.

CONSOMME À LA TOLEDO—CLEAR SOUP.
MISS STEVENSON.

One quart stock, two eggs, two gherkins, a little red and green colouring, two tablespoonfuls cream, whites and shells of two eggs, one wine glass of sherry, and a little nutmeg. Beat the two whole eggs, pour over them the cream (hot.) Season the custard with pepper, salt and nutmeg, colour half red and half green, pour both parts into buttered tins, poach in hot water until firm. Beat the whites and shells of eggs with a little cold water, add them to the stock, pour it into a saucepan and whisk over the fire till boiling; draw on one side and simmer ten minutes. Cut the custard in shapes, rinse then in warm water, shred the gherkins, strain the soup, add the wine and garnishing just before serving.

CAULIFLOWER SOUP.

One cauliflower, two yolks of egg, one half pint of cream, one quart chicken stock. Boil together the stock and cauliflower, for twenty minutes, take out the cauliflower, put aside some of the best parts, pass remainder through a sieve, mix together the yolks and cream, add them to the soup, put all in a saucepan and stir over the fire until it begins to thicken, put the pieces of cauliflower into a tureen and pour the soup over them; the stock used in this soup is better without any other vegetables.

FISH SOUP.

Two pounds of raw fish, one tablespoonful parsley, one and one half ounces butter, one ounce flour of rice, one half pint milk, one quart of water, pepper, and salt. Boil together the bones and skin of fish for half an hour. Strain, melt butter in a saucepan, stir into it the flour, add strained water from the pan. Cut up the fish into small pieces, add it, also salt and pepper, boil slowly ten minutes, add parsley at last minute.

GIBLET SOUP.
MISS BEEMER.

Giblets from two or three fowls; two quarts of water; one of stock; two tablespoons of butter, ditto of flour; salt, pepper, and onion if desired. Put giblets on to boil in the water and boil gently till reduced to one quart (about two hours); take out the giblets, cut off tough parts and chop fine the remainder. Return to the liquor and add stock. Cook butter and flour together until a rich brown, and add to the soup; season, cook gently half an hour; stir in half a cup of bread crumbs and in a few minutes serve hot.

KIDNEY SOUP.
MISS STEVENSON.

One ox kidney, one quart second stock or water, one tablespoon Hardy sauce, one tablespoon mushroom ketchup, one ounce butter, one ounce rice flour, pepper, salt and cayenne. Wash and dry the kidney, cut into thin slices; mix together the flour, pepper and salt and roll the kidney in it. Brown them quickly in the butter, pour over the stock, skim when boiling. Add sauce and simmer slowly two hours.

LENTIL SOUP.
MRS. THEOPHILUS OLIVER.

One half pound of lentils, one carrot, one onion, one ounce dripping, salt, pepper corns, one quart of water, one tablespoon of flour. Soak the lentils all night, wash well, scrape carrot, and onion cut up. Put the dripping into a saucepan, when warm, put in vegetables, lentils and flour. Stir for five minutes until all fat is absorbed, add the water warm, some herbs tied in a bit of muslin. Boil for an hour or more. Rub through a sieve, return to saucepan. Reheat and serve.

OX TAIL SOUP.
MRS. W. COOK.

Divide an ox tail into lengths of an inch and a half; melt an ounce of butter in a stew pan and fry the pieces in this, turning them about for five minutes. Add two quarts of stock or water and bring gently to a boil. Throw in a teaspoonful of salt, and carefully remove the scum as it rises. Add a carrot, a turnip and an onion with two cloves stuck in it, a little celery, a blade of mace and a small bouquet of garum. Stew gently two and one half hours. Strain the soup and put the pieces of ox tail in cold water to free them of fat. Mix an ounce and one half of flour smoothly with a little cold water, add to the stock and simmer for twenty minutes. Add a little cayenne, a few drops of lemon juice and a glass of port wine if liked and serve.

OYSTER SOUP.

MISS MIRIAM STRANG.

One quart boiling water, one quart milk, stir in one teacup rolled cracker crumbs, season with pepper and salt to taste. When all come to a boil add one quart of oysters; stir well so as to keep from scorching, then add a piece of butter size of an egg; let it boil up just once, then remove from the fire immediately.

CREAM OF PEA SOUP.

MISS RUTH SCOTT.

One tin of peas and one pint of water, a very small piece of onion, let it boil about twenty minutes, strain and mash through sieve. Two tablespoonfuls of butter, and one of flour, well blended together. Add that to the peas. Last of all add a pint or *more of boiling milk*. Put on the stove till it thickens, but be careful not to let it boil.

PALESTINE SOUP.

MRS. W. COOK.

Wash and pare two pounds of artichokes and put them in a stewpan with a slice of butter, two or three strips of bacon rind, which have been scalded and scraped and two bay leaves. Put the lid on the stew pan and let the vegetables "sweat" over the fire for eight or ten minutes, shaking the pan occasionally to keep them from sticking. Pour on water to cover the artichokes and stew gently till soft. Rub them through a sieve, mix the liquor they were boiled in with them, make the soup hot and add boiling milk until it is as thick as double cream. Add pepper and salt to taste. Just before serving, mix with the soup a quarter of a pint of hot cream. This addition will be a valuable one, but may be dispensed with.

PUREE DE PETIT POIS.

MISS STEVENSON.

One pint green peas, two yolks of egg, one gill cream, one and one half pints stock, salt and pepper. Strain the liquid from the peas, put them with the stock in a saucepan and simmer twenty minutes; pass them through a sieve, pour back to the pan, add yolks, cream, pepper and salt, and stir over the fire until it begins to thicken; do not allow it to boil. A spray of mint boiled with the peas is a great improvement.

PUREE DE VEAU.

Four ounces pounded veal, one pint stock, one ounce butter, one ounce flour, yolks of two eggs, few drops of lemon juice, one half pint whipped cream. Mix veal and butter together in a saucepan, add flour, then by degrees the stock (hot) just boil up. Mix yolks and add little by little the cream, a few drops of cochineal, salt and pepper, pour over this the contents of the saucepan very carefully.

TOMATO SOUP.
MRS. HENRY THOMSON.

One pint of stewed tomatoes, add a pinch of soda, stir till it ceases foaming, then add one pint boiling water and one pint of milk, strain and put on the stove and when near boiling, add a tablespoonful of cornstarch, wet it with a little cold milk, one tablespoon butter, a little pepper and salt to taste.

TOMATO SOUP.
MISS EDITH HENRY.

Take a tin of tomatoes and add half a pint of water. Let this boil for half an hour till the tomatoes are well broken. Add a tablespoonful of cornstarch, dissolved in a little cold water and mix well. Flavor with salt and pepper to taste, and half a small onion. Then add a quart of milk. Let this boil and stir well, so that it will mix, and be careful that it does not burn on the bottom of the pan.

TURKISH SOUP.
MRS. W. COOK.

One quart of white stock, one half teacupful of rice, yolks of two eggs, one tablespoon cream, salt and pepper. In preparing this soup boil first the rice in the stock for twenty minutes. Then pass the whole through a wire sieve, rubbing through such of the rice as may stick with a spoon, then stir it thoroughly to beat out such lumps as the rice may have formed and return all to the saucepan. The yolk of egg, cream, pepper and salt, must now be well beaten together and added to the stock and rice, the whole stirred over the fire for two minutes, care being taken to prevent boiling after the eggs are put in, or they will curdle. This soup should be served very hot and is excellent.

TURTLE BEAN SOUP.
MISS FRASER.

One pint of black beans, boil in two quarts of water, one onion, two carrots, small teaspoon of allspice, five or six cloves, a small bit of bacon or ham. A good bone of roast beef or mutton, let all boil till quite tender perhaps two hours. Then turn into a colander, take out the bone and rub all the rest with a wooden spoon through the colander, if this is too thick add some stock or water. Some meat balls can be added.

FISH AND OYSTERS.

"Now good digestion wait on appetite,
And health on both." —MACBETH.

RULE FOR SELECTING FISH.

If the gills are red, the eyes full, and the whole fish firm and stiff, they are fresh and good; if on the contrary, the gills are pale, the eyes sunken, the flesh flabby, they are stale.

BAKED CODFISH.
MRS. DAVID BELL.

Choose a good sized fresh codfish, prepare it for cooking without beheading it, fill the inside with a dressing of bread crumbs, a finely chopped onion, a little chopped suet, pepper and salt and moisten all with an egg. Sew up the fish and bake, basting with butter or dripping. If butter, beware of too much salt.

BAKED CODFISH.
MRS. R. M. STOCKING.

Pick very fine one cup of codfish; soak several hours in cold water; have ready two cups of mashed potatoes and mix well with one egg, a cup of milk, one half cup of butter, little salt and pepper; put this in a baking dish and cover the top with bread crumbs; moisten with milk; bake one-half hour.

CURRIED FISH.
MRS. W. COOK.

One pound cooked white fish, one apple, two ounces of butter, one onion, one pint of fish stock, one tablespoon curry-powder, one tablespoon flour, one teaspoon lemon juice or vinegar, salt and pepper, six ounces of rice. Slice the apple and onion, and brown them in a pan with a little butter, stir in them the flour and curry powder, add the stock by degrees; skim when boiling and simmer slowly one half hour, stir in them the lemon juice, also a very small teaspoon sugar; strain and return to the saucepan, cut up the fish into neat pieces, and put them into the saucepan also, when quite hot dish with a border of rice.

FISH CREAM.

MRS. J. G. SCOTT.

One can of salmon, one quart of milk, one cup of flour, one cup of butter, three eggs, one cupful of bread crumbs, one half cupful grated cheese, one onion, one bunch of parsley, two bay leaves. Take the canned salmon, or boil a fish, and when cool take out the bones and break the fish in small pieces. Put on to boil one quart of milk, an onion, a bunch of parsley, and two bay leaves; after boiling strain through a colander, then add a cup of flour mixed smooth with cold milk and a cup of butter; beat up three eggs and pour into the mixture. Put in a baking dish alternate layers of fish and cream until the dish is full, putting cream top and bottom. Place on top one cup of bread crumbs and one half cup of grated cheese. Salt to taste, and cayenne pepper. Bake twenty minutes.

FISH MOULD.

MRS. A. COOK.

Boil a fresh haddock, remove the bones and pick it in pieces, soak some bread in milk; put the fish, bread, a small piece of butter, one or two eggs, pepper and salt together in a bowl and beat them well together. Put the mixture in a mould and steam, turn out, and garnish with parsley. Tomato sauce is nice poured round the mould when turned out. The fish should be about twice the quantity of the bread.

TOMATO SAUCE.

Six tomatoes, two ounces butter, one half ounce flour, one half pint stock, one teaspoon of salt, one fourth teaspoon of pepper. Place the tomatoes in a pan and pour over them the stock, add salt and pepper. Place the pan over the fire and cook all slowly for half an hour. Place a wire sieve over a basin and rub the tomatoes and stock through the sieve. Melt the butter in a saucepan, add the flour stir well together, pour over the tomatoes and stock and stir all over the fire till boiling, when the sauce is ready for use. Tinned tomatoes do not take so long to boil.

FISH SCALLOP.

MISS RUTH SCOTT.

Remains of cold fish of any sort, one half pint of cream, one half tablespoonful anchovy sauce, one half teaspoonful made mustard, one half teaspoonful walnut ketchup, pepper and salt, bread crumbs. Put all the ingredients into a stew pan, carefully picking the fish from the bones; set it on the fire, let it remain till nearly hot, and stir occasionally. Then put in a deep dish, with bread and small bits of butter on top; put in the oven till nearly browned. Serve hot.

FISH PIE.

MRS. ANDREW THOMSON.

Boil one haddock, take the best part of the fish, one pint of milk and a piece of butter as large as an egg, half a cup of flour, two yolks of eggs, stir together, and then mix well with the fish. Put in a pudding dish, and take a half cup of bread crumbs, half a cup of grated cheese, put in the oven for ten minutes, salt and pepper to taste.

POTTED HERRINGS.
MRS. DAVID BELL.

Scale and clean fresh herrings, then taking the fish by the tail you can easily remove the backbone drawing it towards the head. The smaller bones will melt in the vinegar; remove the heads and roll each fish up, tail end inside, and wind a thread round each roll, lay them in the vessel they are to remain in till used, a stone earthernware crock is best. Make scalding hot with spices as much vinegar as will cover them, pour it over the fish and keep them hot about the stove for about an hour, when they will be well cooked through; do not let them boil or they will break. Keep in a cool place. Spices: whole white pepper, whole allspice, and a blade of mace if it is liked.

LOBSTER CUTLETS.
MRS. FARQUHARSON SMITH.

Mince the lobster fine, and season with pepper and salt, make good and thick with drawn butter. Mix with the lobster enough to make it stick together. Shape with the hands into cutlets, roll in bread crumbs and fry in hot lard.

The Sauce:—Make rather a thin custard, season with pepper, salt and a little nutmeg and chopped parsley, place over the cutlets.

LOBSTER STEW.
MRS. ERNEST F. WURTELE.

Take a boiled lobster and split it open, cut the meat into small pieces and put into a saucepan with one pint of milk; when boiling add two tablespoons of flour dissolved in a little water, and boil ten minutes. Season with salt, pepper and a small piece of butter. Just before serving pour in a wineglassful of sherry. Canned lobster may be used with very good results.

OYSTER PIE.—FAMOUS.

One cup melted butter is put in a lined saucepan, and three tablespoons of flour which are rubbed well into the butter, one half teaspoon of mace, a little pepper and salt. The juice of the oysters is put into this to make it thin, and little by little one quart of boiling milk to one quart of oysters. Last the oysters are put in very carefully and given a very short boil. The whole is pretty thick and is then put into a pie dish with pie crust over; one cup of cream is put in just before the oysters are emptied into the pie dish.

OYSTER PIE OR PATTIES.
MISS M. A. RITCHIE.

Crust:—One pound of butter, one pound of flour, one half cup of water. Sauce:—One tablespoonful of butter, two tablespoonfuls of flour, one cup of cream or milk, one pint of oysters.

ESCALOPED OYSTERS.

MADAME J. T.

Butter the dish; cover the bottom of the dish with bread crumbs, add a layer of oysters, season with pepper and salt, then bread crumbs and oysters until you have three layers. Finish with crumbs, cover the top with small pieces of butter, bake half an hour.

CREAMED OYSTERS ON TOAST.

MRS. R. M. STOCKING.

One quart of milk, two tablespoons flour three tablespoons butter, pepper and salt. Put milk in double boiler, mix butter and flour thoroughly, adding a little cold milk before stirring into the hot milk; cook: One pint of oysters, let simmer in their liquor for about five minutes, then skim out, drop into the cream sauce. Prepare thin slices of crisp toast, lay on heated platter; pour over creamed oysters, serve at once. Delicious.

OYSTER CROQUETTES.

MISS STEVENSON.

Twenty-five oysters, one dessertspoonful chopped parsley, three ounces butter, one and one half ounces flour, one gill milk or cream, one teaspoon lemon juice, one egg, three tablespoons bread crumbs, salt and pepper. Boil the oysters in their own liquor five minutes, cut them in rough pieces, melt the butter in a saucepan, stir in the flour, add cream by degrees, also oyster liquor, boil two minutes, add then the parsley, pepper, and salt, put in the oysters and allow the mixture to cool. Form it then into croquettes on a slightly floured board. Roll in the beaten egg and bread crumbs and fry in hot fat two minutes.

MOULDED SALMON.

MISS MARION STOWELL POPE.

One tin of salmon chopped, one cup fine bread crumbs, four eggs broken in four tablespoons melted butter, one teaspoon chopped parsley, pepper and salt to taste. Put into a plain buttered mould and sprinkle with flour, cover and steam one hour.

Sauce for the above:—One teaspoon cornstarch, a little butter, one and one half cups of milk, pepper, salt and nutmeg to taste. A little tomato ketchup or anchovy sauce added. When it comes to the boil, add one well beaten egg; pour round the mould and serve hot.

CREAMED SALMON.

MISS H. BARCLAY.

One can salmon minced fine, draw off the liquor. For the dressing, boil one pint milk, two tablespoons butter, salt and pepper to taste. Have ready one pint of bread crumbs, place a layer in the bottom of the dish, then a layer of fish, then a layer of dressing, and so on, leaving crumbs for the last layer, and bake till brown.

MEATS.

MEATS.
MRS. DAVID BELL.

To make beefsteak tender, rub a pinch of baking soda on each side of the steak about an hour before cooking and roll it up on itself in the meantime. A very small pinch of brown sugar used in the same way is good, but the soda is thought preferable.

MEAT BALLS.
MRS. WADDLE.

Mash finely some potatoes, pass through a sieve, stir in the yolks of two eggs, one ounce of butter, pepper and salt. Mince finely some beef or tongue. Mix all well together, add a little parsley, roll into balls, cover with egg and bread crumbs, fry in hot lard. Let them dry before the fire on paper. Very good.

SPICED BEEF.

Rub well into a round weighing forty pounds, three ounces saltpetre, let stand six or eight hours, pound three ounces allspice, one pound black pepper, two pounds salt, and seven ounces brown sugar; rub the beef well with the salt and spices. Let it remain fourteen days turning it every day and rub with the pickle, then wash off the spices and put in a deep pan, cut small six pounds of suet, put some in the bottom of the pan, the greater part on the top, cover with coarse paste and bake eight hours; when cold take off the paste pour off the gravy, it will keep six months.

SPICED BEEF.
MISS J. E. FRASER.

Two pounds of raw steak from the round, free from bone, fat or sinew, chopped very fine, six soda biscuits rolled fine, one cup of milk, two eggs beaten in one tablespoon salt, one dessertspoon of pepper, and add a little spice if you like. Butter an earthenware jar as large round the top as the bottom and press the mixture in very lightly. Cover with butter one half inch thick. Cover the jar with a plate and bake in an oven for two hours. Serve whole or cut in slices. Nicer cold.

BEEF À LA MODE.

MRS. I. T. SMYTHE.

One half pound of meat, cut up into four inch squares and two or three inches thick, add onion chopped fine, one teaspoon salt, and one half teaspoon pepper, cover with boiling water and place in jar and cook in oven for two hours.

BEEF OLIVES.

MRS. GEORGE M. CRAIG.

Thin slices of steak cut into squares about the size of hand; make a dressing similar to chicken, bake, then put on the steak and roll, put in the saucepan with some onion and butter in a little water, let it simmer for an hour and a half to two hours.

COLD MEAT CUTLETS.

MRS. A. COOK.

Half pound cold meat or chicken, one ounce butter, one ounce of flour, one gill white stock, one teaspoon chopped parsley, one half saltspoon grated nutmeg, small teaspoon of salt, saltspoon of pepper, grated rind of half a small lemon. Pass chicken twice through the mincer, then melt the butter, stir into it the flour, get it perfectly smooth and add stock, don't let it brown, stir until it boils and boil two minutes, add the chicken, (when properly cooked will leave the pan clearly) add pepper, salt, nutmeg, parsley and lemon, put it away to cool. In using cold beef, a teaspoon anchovy essence or paste is an improvement, and to mutton a teaspoon mushroom catsup. When the mixture is cold, place some flour on board to prevent sticking and form into rolls with square edges, beat the egg, place breadcrumbs mixed with pepper and salt on paper, put the rolls first in the egg, then in crumbs, have sufficient fat in pan and when the white smoke rises, put the rolls in and fry three minutes, drain on paper. Brown sauce may be served and mashed peas or potatoes placed in the centre.

CURED MUTTON HAMS.

MRS. W. COOK.

Quarter of a pound bay salt, ditto of common salt, one ounce saltpetre, four ounces brown sugar, one ounce allspice, four ounces black pepper (whole), the allspice or one ounce of coriander seed must be bruised not ground, one quart of water: boil all together a few minutes and rub on hot. In three weeks the hams will be ready to hang if well rubbed with the pickle everyday. Sufficient pickle for two.

BRAISED MUTTON.

MRS. ARCHIE COOK.

One boned shoulder of mutton, four ounces of bread crumbs, two ounces of suet, rind of half a lemon, bunch of mixed vegetables, one tablespoon chopped parsley, other herbs if liked, one egg, a little milk, one teaspoon of salt, half teaspoon of pepper. Chop suet finely (or fat from mutton will do) add breadcrumbs, parsley, grated lemon rind and salt, moisten with egg and milk. Place mixture in mutton, roll up and tie securely. Slice vegetables and put them with bones in saucepan also two cloves, a bay leaf and peppercorns, pour over them a pint of stock or water, place mutton on top and boil slowly about one and one half hours according to size of meat, then brush it over with glaze or sprinkle with flour, pepper and salt and bake it half an hour. Place on a dish, pour fat from pan and stir in half ounce of flour (browned) add stock in which meat was cooked, also one tablespoon mushroom catsup and one tablespoon Worcester sauce, pepper and salt, boil two minutes and strain around meat. Vegetables in stock can be cut to ornament the dish.

GENUINE IRISH STEW.

MRS. DUNCAN LAURIE.

Take the feet and legs of a pig, cut off at the hams, two will be sufficient for a family of eight. Singe off the hair and thoroughly cleanse them, removing the toes by scorching. Cut the legs in pieces suitable for stewing, put down in cold water and cook slowly for three hours. Pare and cut up nine or ten good sized potatoes and add to your stew with salt and pepper, about one half an hour before dishing. After the potatoes have been put in, the greatest care must be taken to prevent them from sticking to the pot and burning, therefore you must stir frequently with a spoon. What remains from dinner pour into a mould and it will become a jelly, which is nice eaten cold for breakfast.

TO STEW A FRESH TONGUE.

MRS. ARCHIE COOK.

Wash it very well and rub it well with common salt and a little saltpetre; let it lie two or three days; then boil till the skin will peel off; put it into a saucepan with part of the liquor it has boiled in and a pint of good stock, season with black and Jamaica pepper, two or three pounded cloves. Add a glassful of white wine, a tablespoonful of mushroom catsup and one of lemon pickle, thicken with butter rolled in flour. Stew the tongue till quite soft in this sauce; the wine can be added when dished or left out if preferred.

LAMBS' TONGUES STEWED.

MRS. ARCHIE COOK.

Six tongues, three heaping tablespoons of butter, one large onion, two slices of carrot, three slices of white turnip, three tablespoons flour, one of salt, a little pepper, one quart of stock or water and some sweet herbs. Boil the tongues one hour and a half in clear water, take them up, cover with cold water, and draw off the skins. Put the butter, onion, turnip and carrot in the stewpan and cook slowly for fifteen minutes, then add the flour and cook until brown, stirring all the time. Stir the stock into this and when it boils up, add the tongues, salt, pepper and herbs;

simmer gently for two hours. Cut the carrots, turnips and potatoes into cubes. Boil the potatoes in salted water ten minutes and the carrots and turnips one hour. Place the tongues in the centre of a hot dish, arrange the vegetables around them, strain the gravy, over all. Garnish with parsley.

ROAST FILLET OF VEAL.

MRS. RATTRAY.

Take a good sized, white, fat leg of veal, weighing some ten or twelve pounds. Remove the meat carefully from the bone and take out the bone. Then pin the meat securely into a nice round with skewers; fill the cavity from which the bone was taken with the following dressing. Roast in a slow oven, allowing one quarter of an hour for each pound, and be sure to keep it thoroughly basted with plenty of beef dripping.

DRESSING.

Make ready one coffee cup of bread crumbs, one teaspoonful of chopped parsley, one half teaspoonful summer savory, pepper and salt to taste. Take a good sized onion, peel, slice, and fry it well with a piece of butter the size of an egg; pour the liquor from this into your bread crumbs and blend all thoroughly together. Be careful not to put the onion in, only the fried butter and onion juice. When the meat is cooked, remove from pan and make a rich brown gravy to serve with it. Garnish your dish with fried bacon and slices of lemon.

STUFFING FOR VEAL.

MRS. W. CLINT.

Chop half a pound of beef suet very fine, put in a basin, with eight ounces of bread crumbs, four ounces of chopped parsley, a tablespoonful of equal quantities of powdered thyme and marjoram, the rind of a lemon grated, the juice of half a one; season with pepper and salt, and a quarter of a nutmeg; mix the whole with two eggs; this will do also for turkey or baked fish.

YORKSHIRE PUDDING.

MRS. GEORGE CRESSMAN.

Two eggs, four tablespoonfuls of flour, a little salt and milk to make a batter the thickness of cream. When the beef is roasted pour off the boiling dripping into another pan, turn in the batter and bake to a good brown.

GAME.

ACCOMPANIMENTS.—With wild ducks, cucumber sauce, currant jelly or cranberry sauce.

ROAST DUCK WITH APPLES.
MISS BEEMER.

Pluck and singe a duck, draw it without breaking the intestines, wipe it with a wet towel and lay it in a baking pan; wipe a dozen small sour apples with a wet cloth, cut out the cores without breaking the apples, and arrange them around the duck; put the pan into a hot oven and quickly brown the duck, then moderate the heat of the oven and continue the cooking for about twenty minutes, or until the apples are tender but not broken, baste both duck and apples every five minutes until they are done, and then serve them on the same dish. It is a great improvement some think, to parboil the duck for fifteen minutes with an onion in the water, and the strong fishy flavor that is sometimes so disagreeable in wild ducks will have disappeared. A carrot will answer the same purpose.

ROAST QUAIL WITH BREAD SAUCE.

Peel and slice an onion and put it over the fire in a pint of milk; pluck and singe half a dozen quail, draw them without breaking the intestines, cut off the heads and feet, and wipe them with a wet towel; rub them all over with butter; season them with pepper and salt, and roast them before a very hot fire for fifteen minutes basting them three or four times with butter. Have some slices of toast laid under them to catch the drippings. While the birds are roasting make a bread sauce as follows; roll a pint bowlfull of dry bread, and sift the crumbs; use the finest ones for the sauce, and the largest for the frying later; remove the onion from the milk in which it has been boiling, stir into the milk the finest portion of the crumbs, season it with a saltspoonful of white pepper and a grate of nutmeg, stir in a tablespoonful of butter, and stir the sauce until it is smooth; then place the saucepan containing it in a pan of boiling water to keep it hot; put two tablespoonfuls of butter over the fire in a frying pan, and when it is smoking hot put into it the coarse half of the crumbs, dust them with cayenne pepper, and stir them until they are light brown; then at once put them on a hot dish; put the bread sauce into a gravy-boat ready to send it to the table. Arrange to have the fried breadcrumbs, sauce and quail done at the same time; serve the birds on the toast which has been laid under them; in serving the quail, lay each bird on a hot plate, pour over it a large spoonful of the bread sauce and on that place a spoonful of the fried bread crumbs.

VENISON STEAK.
MRS. ERNEST F. WURTELE.

Take a piece of frozen venison, and put into water in which has been put two tablespoons of vinegar. Just leave until the ice comes to the surface of the meat, take the meat out and remove the ice with a knife; wipe dry and flour well, put a good piece of butter in the pan; let brown, put the steak in salt, and pepper, fry on both sides, then add a cup of rich milk, push the pan to the back of the stove and cover it and let it stew slowly for one and a half hours—If the steak is very dry lard it with salt pork before frying.

STEWED PIGEONS.
MRS. HARRY LAURIE.

For two pair of pigeons stuff first with bread, summer savory, butter, pepper, salt. Put eight or nine slices of fat pork, in an iron pot to fry, until the pork is well browned, then take it out and put in the pigeons and let brown thoroughly, keep turning to prevent burning. Then add one pint of stock, season if required, put back slices of pork and let stew for an hour and a half (at least) quietly. If gravy is not thick enough, add a tablespoon of brown flour. About quarter of an hour before done, put in a can of green peas—Then serve.

STEWED HARE.

Can be prepared in the same manner as the above for stewed pigeons, with the addition of spices: cloves a few, and a little more of cinnamon.

BREAD SAUCE.
MRS. BENSON BENNETT.

One half pint boiled milk to one cup of fine bread crumbs, one small onion, two cloves, one piece of mace, salt to taste, let simmer five minutes, add small piece of butter.

CRANBERRY JELLY.

Pare, quarter, and core twelve good sized tart apples, place in a porcelain kettle with two quarts of cranberries, cover well with cold water and stew until soft, then strain through a jelly bag, add to this juice two pounds of confectioner's sugar, and boil as you would any other jelly, until it falls from the skimmer; when you dip it in skim off any froth that arises while boiling, put in moulds and let it get firm before using.

PLAIN DRESSING FOR FOWLS.
MRS. W. CLINT.

One cup and a half of bread crumbs (not too stale), one heaped teaspoon each of parsley, thyme and savory, one dessert spoonful butter, half teaspoon salt, quarter of a teaspoon pepper, mix all together with a little milk.

PLAIN DRESSING FOR GEESE AND DUCKS.

One cup breadcrumbs or potatoes, one cup or more of stewed onions, one tablespoon sage, pepper, salt and a little butter, mix with a little milk.

VEGETABLES.

"Cheerful cooks make every dish a feast."

—MASSINGER.

Always have the water boiling when you put your vegetables in, and keep it constantly boiling until they are done. Cook each kind by itself when convenient. All vegetables should be well seasoned.

APPLES.
MRS. DAVID BELL.

When the barrel of apples you have bought, begins to make your mind uneasy, because they can spoil faster than you can use them, a good plan is to peel, core and stir them with a very little sugar and screw them down in your jam jars. They will keep for a couple of months and will be handy to fill a tart or as apple sauce, etc.; they do not need to be cooked too much and some of the firmer sorts may remain in quarters solid enough for a pie. Another plan is to peel but not core the suspicious ones, then let them freeze solid, when frozen pack them in a box and cover. Keep them where they will not thaw. When you wish for a dish of baked apples, put them in your baking pan, scatter a little sugar over them and put them in a quick oven without letting them thaw, when done, they should each be whole and a pretty brown color.

BEANS.

Beans are a nice winter vegetable, but cooked with pork as "baked beans," are too strong for daily use, but are a desirable article of food cooked more plainly. Choose the small white beans, put them in a saucepan with as much cold water, as will cover them well and a small pinch of baking soda; when they have simmered a few minutes drain off the water and replace it with hot water and a little salt; if possible let them cook without boiling hard; when tender drain, and dish with a liberal piece of butter and a dust of pepper. They are also good thrown when drained into the frying pan with some dripping, pepper and salt, and heated a few minutes over the fire. The only attention they require in cooking is lest they melt into soup when nearly cooked.

FRIED BEETS.
MRS. DUNCAN LAURIE.

Boil until tender, slice and put in stewpan with a teaspoon of vinegar, half the juice of a lemon, one half teaspoonful each sugar and salt, a grate of nutmeg and a dash of pepper. Add two tablespoonfuls of stock, a teaspoon butter, and let simmer one half hour.

CREAMED CABBAGE.

MISS J. E. FRASER.

Cut a medium sized cabbage in quarters. Take out the stem, put into a kettle of boiling water, cook for ten minutes, drain and cover with cold water. This will destroy the odor so unpleasant. When cold, chop fine, season with salt and pepper. Make a sauce of two tablespoons of butter, one tablespoon flour, mix smooth, add one pint of milk; cook in this sauce slowly for three quarters of an hour.

STEWED CUCUMBERS.

MRS. DAVID BELL.

Peel a nice straight cucumber, cut in four lengthwise, scoop out all seeds, and cut it in pieces about three inches long; throw these into a saucepan of boiling water with a little salt. When they bend under the touch, they are done, drain in a sieve, then put in a stewpan with a good sized piece of butter, finely chopped parsley salt and pepper. Toss over the fire till thoroughly heated through and serve in a hot dish.

OYSTER CABBAGE.

MRS. D. M. COOK.

Mince fine one half a cabbage, boil for ten minutes and strain off water. Then cover cabbage with milk and let come to a boil, add rolled cracker crumbs, butter size of a walnut, salt and pepper to taste.

CORN OMELET.

Boil one half dozen ears of corn, cut corn from the cob; beat four eggs separately, add to the corn the beaten yolks, salt and pepper, put in the whites last, fry in a pan with plenty of butter.

MACARONI AND CHEESE.

MISS H. BARCLAY.

Boil quarter of a pound of macaroni in water, for half an hour, cool and chop. Make a sauce of one tablespoonful butter, one dessertspoon of flour, half pint milk, one teaspoonful of mustard. Boil one minute; mix all together with three ounces of grated cheese. Put in a shallow dish sprinkling top with cheese. Bake a golden brown and garnish with toast.

MACARONI.

MRS. THOM.

One half pound macaroni, one half pound cheese, one quarter pound of butter, pint of milk, mustard and cayenne. Boil macaroni in salt and water until tender, drain and lay in dish. Put pint of milk on fire, just before boiling, add one tablespoon flour, rubbed smooth in a little cold milk, butter, nearly all the cheese grated, mustard and cayenne. Boil until thick as custard, then pour over macaroni, sprinkle remainder of cheese on top with some small pieces of butter; if used immediately bake twenty minutes, if allowed to get cold one half hour.

CREAM-BAKED ONIONS.

MRS. J. S. THOM.

Pare as many good-sized onions as required and cover with boiling water, boil for ten minutes, then drain. Cover again with boiling water to which add one half teaspoon of salt, and cook till tender. Drain carefully and put the onions in a baking dish, place on each a teaspoon of butter, add pepper and salt to taste, then fill the dish half full of milk and cover with a layer of fine bread-crumbs. Bake till a delicate brown.

CORN OYSTERS.

MRS. FRANK GLASS.

One pint green grated corn, two tablespoons of milk, two eggs, two tablespoons of butter, flour to make a batter. Fry with butter.

OYSTER PANCAKES.

MRS. WADDLE.

One quart of new milk, three eggs, one half dozen green corn grated, one half teacup melted butter, one teaspoon salt and pepper. Flour enough to make a thin batter, fry with butter.

STIRRED POTATOES WITH EGGS.

MISS GRACE MACMILLAN.

Eight cold boiled potatoes chopped fine. Put into the saucepan a piece of butter the size of an egg. When it melts stir in the potatoes, stirring them till brown, then pour in four well beaten eggs, and stir them well through the potatoes. Serve very hot.

SWEET POTATOES STUFFED.

MRS. ARCHIBALD LAURIE.

Four large sized sweet potatoes baked until tender, then cut carefully in two. Cut a piece off each end, so they will stand, then scoop out, leaving the skins perfect. Mash the potato fine with an egg dressing as follows: boil four eggs hard, mash the yolks to a paste with cream to thin, salt and pepper to taste and a little mustard if liked; with this mixture fill the skins, place a piece of butter on top of each, and bake until well browned. Serve in individual saucers with a small doyley under.

POTATO FRILL.
MRS. FRANK GLASS.

Boil and mash some potatoes, working in a little milk and butter but not enough to make the paste soft; while hot add one beaten egg. Shape this paste into a fence on the inside round of a shallow dish, fluting it with the round handle of a knife. Set one minute in a hot oven but not long enough to cause the fence to crack. Glaze quickly with butter and pour the meat carefully within the wall. The mince should not be so thin as to wash away the frill.

POTATO PUFF.
MISS CORDELIA JACKSON.

Take two cupfuls of cold mashed potato, and stir into it six teaspoonfuls of melted butter, beating to a white cream before adding anything else. Then put with this two eggs, whipped very light and a teacupful of cream or milk, salting to taste. Beat all well, pour into a deep dish, and bake in a quick oven until it is nicely browned. If properly mixed it will come out of the oven light, puffy and delectable.

POTATO PEARS.
MRS. J. S. THOM

Boil six or eight large potatoes, when well done mash thoroughly, adding a little butter, cream, pepper and salt. Mould into shape of pears, putting a clove into stem and brush over with beaten egg, and put into the oven to brown slightly.

POTATO FRICASSÉ.
MRS. J. T. SMYTHE.

Cut into thin slices one half pound of fat salt pork. Place in stewpan, when brown, add an onion sliced and a little cold water, cook a few minutes. Cut up a number of good sized potatoes, add this to onion and pork and one half teaspoon of pepper. Cover well with cold water. Let this boil hard for hours. If about half an hour before serving, it is found not to be thick enough, take off cover and boil until it does thicken.

PEAS WITH CREAM SAUCE.
MRS. STOCKING.

Put one quart of peas in a kettle of salted boiling water and cook fifteen minutes; drain, put a tablespoon of butter in a saucepan, add a tablespoon of flour, mix; add a cup of milk; stir constantly until boiling; add salt, pepper and then the peas; stand over boiling water about five minutes and serve as garnish to baked, broiled or fried sweetbreads.

CREAMED RICE.

MRS. LAWRENCE.

Two thirds cup raw rice, one quart of milk, one half cup sugar, flavor with grated rind of lemon or nutmeg. Cook in a pie dish in moderate oven for one and half hour.

TO BOIL RICE.

MISS M. SAMPSON.

Have enough boiling water with a pinch of salt to more than cover the rice, boil for twenty minutes, do not stir, strain through a collander when cooked, and serve.

SPINACH ON TOAST.

MRS. FRANK GLASS.

Cook twenty minutes in boiling salted water. Drain and chop fine. Put a tablespoon of butter into a saucepan with a teaspoon of sugar, a pinch of nutmeg, pepper and salt. Stir in the spinach and beat smooth while it heats; at the last, add one tablespoonful of cream or two of milk. Pour upon crustless slices of buttered toast laid upon a flat dish.

VEGETABLE MARROW.

MRS. DAVID BELL.

Cut in slices half an inch thick, peel and remove the spongy portion; fry in hot dripping or butter, pepper and salt; also nice to make a light batter and dip the slices in, afterwards frying a golden brown.

ENTRÉES AND MEATS RÉCHAUFFÉ.

BEEF CROQUETTES.
MISS FRANCIS FRY.

Two cups beef (minced fine), one cup stock, two pounds flour, one pound butter, one teaspoon lemon juice or vinegar, ditto of onion and salt, one half teaspoon pepper, two eggs, bread or biscuit crumbs. Make a thick sauce by cooking flour and butter; add gradually stock and lemon juice, season; add chopped meat with the onion and one egg. Cook five minutes and turn out to cool. Form into shape roll in beaten egg and crumbs, and fry in boiling lard.

CREAM OF CHICKEN.
MRS. ARCHIE COOK.

Pound three quarters of a pound of chicken, veal or rabbit until quite smooth, then pound one half pound of panada (bread soaked in hot milk), and mix the two together, add two tablespoonfuls of thick soubise sauce, an ounce and a quarter butter, two tablespoons sherry, a little pepper and salt and three whole eggs. Pass the mixture through a fine wire sieve and then add two tablespoons of thick cream. Butter some small timbale moulds and fill them with the mixture, remembering to hit the moulds on the table after having put the mixture into them and steam them about fifteen minutes. Turn them out carefully and serve hot. Tomato sauce poured around them is an improvement. If preferred they can be cold and decorated with aspic jelly and a ragout made of truffles, cooked tongue, or ham and button mushrooms, or a little tomato salad could be used.

SOUBISE SAUCE.

Put some onions to soak for ten minutes in boiling water. Peel them, cut in halves or quarters. Put them in a small saucepan with a lump of fresh butter; simmer very slowly until the onions are quite cooked, add salt to taste; thicken with flour, or flour and fine bread crumbs, and add cream or milk. Pass through a sieve, must be thick and smooth. Some people like a pinch of sugar.

JELLIED CHICKEN.
MRS. ARCHIBALD LAURIE.

Take an old fowl, boil until so tender the bones will leave the meat; set aside to cool: next day skim off the fat and boil down to one quart, to this add one ounce of sheet gelatine previously steeped in a little cold water. Pepper and salt to taste, with a little ground savory. Put the meat in a pie dish and by degrees add the liquid to avoid having the meat all in one place. This should turn out well when cold.

MAKE A DOZEN CHICKEN CROQUETTES.

MRS. ANDREW THOMSON.

White of two chickens well minced, one wineglass of sherry, one half pint of cream, pepper and salt and a little cayenne to taste, mix well and put into a buttered mould; steam for one hour.

CHICKEN MOULD. (SERVED COLD.)

MADAME J. T.

Put over one large chicken in a pint and a half of cold water, with a medium sized onion, three stalks of celery, and a small bunch parsley. Let simmer gently (not boil), for two hours. Then remove chicken, pick the meat from the bones, and cut into pieces about an inch long. Put the bones back into the broth and let this boil down to three quarters of a pint. Add gradually two cups cream in which a tablespoonful of flour has been dissolved. When the flour has thickened remove from fire and add two well beaten eggs and a very little nutmeg. Garnish a mould with slices of hard boiled egg and sprigs of parsley. Pour in chicken mixture. Allow to set and serve on lettuce leaves. This will serve eight people.

CURRY. (EXCELLENT.)

MRS. W. COOK.

Take several small onions, chop them up very fine, put them into a pan with a piece of butter, stew them over the fire until the onions are quite dissolved and turned to a light brown. Cut meat into small pieces and rub the curry powder well into the raw meat. Put it into a stew pan with onion and an apple minced fine and a teaspoonful of cream, and let it all simmer for two or three hours. It must not boil.

FISH RÉCHAUFFÉ

One pound cooked fish, one tablespoon each of mushroom ketchup, essence of anchovy, Harvey's sauce and mustard, one ounce of butter, rolled flour and one half a pint of cream, a wall of potatoes. Divide the fish into flakes, place it with cream and butter into a stew pan, until very hot. Mash the potatoes, and add to them one tablespoon cream, one yolk of egg, pepper and salt; well butter a wall mould and sprinkle with browned bread crumbs, and place it in the oven till hot, turn it out on a silver dish and pour the ragoût in the centre. Garnish with lemon and parsley.

FISH CROQUETTES.

MISS FRY.

Mash freshly boiled potatoes, add one egg and flour to make a stiff dough. Roll out thin and cut with a round cutter. Spread on one half the cake chopped fish, mixed with parsley, fold over and press down the edges. Fry in lard.

HOMINY CROQUETTES.
MRS. BENSON BENNETT.

To a cupful of cold boiled hominy, add a tablespoonful of melted butter, and stir, moistening by degrees with a cupful of milk beating to a soft light paste, one teacupful of white sugar, and lastly a well beaten egg. Roll in oval balls with floured hands in egg and bread crumbs and fry in hot lard.

POTTED HEAD.
MISS EDITH M. HENRY.

Take the shank (lower), of meat, cover with water, boil until tender enough to cut up in dice, take off and cut the meat into dice, then throw back into pot, flavor with pepper, salt, mace, celery seed, cayenne pepper, allspice and cloves. Then have ready a little gelatine, mix all through well and let boil a short time, then pour into a cold shape.

KEGEREE.
MRS. BENSON BENNETT.

One teacup of freshly boiled rice, one half quarter of boiled salmon, two soft boiled eggs, lump of butter, salt and pepper. Mix all together and put it in a mould to steam.

DEVILLED LIVER.
MRS. HENRY THOMSON.

To three pounds of uncooked liver, one quarter of a pound of uncooked salt pork, one half pint of bread crumbs, three tablespoons of salt, one teaspoon of pepper, one half a teaspoon each of cayenne pepper, mace and cloves. Mode.—Chop the liver and pork very fine, add the other ingredients mixing well, put it into a covered mould, and set in a saucepan of cold water, cover and place on the fire to cook two hours. Take out the mould, uncover and let it stand in an open oven to let the steam off. This is a cold dish.

MEAT CROQUETTES.
MADAME J. T.

One tablespoon butter, one tablespoon flour, two tablespoon of stock, one tablespoon milk. Let boil until it thickens, then add small teaspoonful onion juice (grated), one teaspoon lemon juice, one small teaspoon lemon rind, pepper and salt, one grate of nutmeg. When well blended, add one beaten up egg, cupful of chopped meat (any kind.) Let this mixture cool in a soup plate and roll into cork shaped croquettes with finely grated bread crumbs and fry in lard hot. Serve on a napkin with parsley and lemon rind.

MOCK PATÉ DE FOIE GRAS.
MRS. BLAIR.

Rub the bottom of a stew-pan five times across with a piece of fresh cut garlic, put in three pounds of larded calf's liver, with two chopped shallots, a laurel leaf, a bay leaf, a blade of mace, four pepper corns, two cloves, a saltspoonful of salt, a saltspoonful of loaf sugar, and half a pint of stock: simmer gently for four hours. Then cut the liver into thin slices, place in a basin, and cover with the liquid: let it remain until next day. Then pound the liver to a paste, add a tablespoonful of salt, a saltspoonful of white pepper; add three quarters of a pound of clarified butter; pound well together and pass through a wire sieve; put into pots; smooth over the top with a knife, then pour over hot clarified butter or lard and keep in a cool place.

POTATO CROQUETTES.
MRS. J. G. SCOTT.

Take two cupfuls of cold mashed potatoes, beat up with two tablespoonfuls of melted butter and three eggs, make into rolls, cover with cracker dust, or bread crumbs and fry.

KIDNEY STEW.
MRS. SEPTIMUS BARROW.

One tablespoon flour, one half tablespoon of salt, one saltspoon pepper, three gills stock or water, one tablespoon mushroom ketchup, two ounces butter or bacon fat. First: Wash the kidney and remove the core—cut into thin slices; mix together pepper, salt and flour, roll kidney in it. Brown it quickly in the butter, then add stock or water; skim well and cook very slowly for two hours.

STEWED SWEETBREADS.
MRS. ERNEST WURTELE.

Soak the sweetbreads in salt and water for twenty minutes, then take them out, wipe them well, and take off the skin. Parboil them for twenty minutes or half an hour, after which you stew them in a little milk, till they are tender, add a little salt and pepper, make a little sauce of the milk and serve. Use a double kettle when stewing.

COLD ENTRÉE.
MRS. FRANK DUGGAN.

An entrée that supplies the want of fish for luncheon. Take the contents of one can of sardines, mince fine with a silver fork removing bits of bone, the tails, etc., etc., add celery salt, pepper and salt to taste, a tablespoonful of lemon juice, a quarter teaspoonful Worcester sauce, a few drops of Harvey's sauce, the same of anchovy sauce. Add a tablespoonful of capers. Mix the whole thoroughly with a little thick cream, (sweet), or mayonnaise. Mould into minature pyramids and serve on lettuce leaves: further garnish the dish with parsley. One can of sardines will be sufficient to make four pyramids. Finely chopped celery may be added before the mayonnaise.

STUFFED TOMATOES (HOT ENTRÉE.)
MRS. JAMES LAURIE.

Six tomatoes, three ounces cooked white meat of any kind, one small shallot, one teaspoon chopped parsley, pepper and salt, two tablespoons bread crumbs, one egg. Take out the centre from the tomatoes; cut the meat into very small pieces, mix with the bread crumbs, parsley, shallot, pepper, salt, and egg. With this fill the tomatoes, put a small piece of butter on each and bake fifteen minutes in a good oven.

MOCK TURKEY.
MRS. HENRY THOMSON.

Three pounds veal, one fourth pound salt pork, finely minced cup bread crumbs (large coffee cup), two eggs, one teaspoonful salt, same of pepper, a little sweet herbs, steam four hours.

TURBOT À LA CRÈME AU GRATIN.
MADAME J. T.

Boil one quart of milk twenty minutes, with one onion, one bunch parsley, one bunch thyme; mix in a little cold milk, one quartercup flour, and add gradually to boiled milk also salt, pepper and a grate of nutmeg. When thick, remove from fire, add one quarter pound fresh butter, the yolks two eggs, and two tablespoonfuls of grated gruyere cheese. Pass through a coarse sieve and pour over two and one half pounds of boiled fish removed from bones and flaked, putting in the dish first a layer of sauce, then a layer of fish, another layer of sauce and another of fish. On top layer put sauce, thickly sprinkled with bread crumbs and grated gruyere cheese. Brown one half an hour in the oven and serve. This quantity will serve ten or twelve people.

JELLIED TONGUE.
MISS MITCHELL.

Take a corned tongue, soak it for twelve hours then boil slowly, pare and skin, and put it in your mould. Have ready half a package of gelatine and a half a thinly cut lemon, place on the tongue and pour your jelly over it. Turn out when cold.

SALADS AND SALAD DRESSING.

"To make a perfect salad, there should be a spendthrift for oil, a miser for vinegar, a wise man for salt, and a madcap to stir the ingredients up, and mix them well together." —SPANISH PROVERB.

APPLE AND CELERY SALAD.
MRS. R. M. STOCKING.

One day at the house of a charming friend,
From dishes of dainty blue,
I ate something good which puzzled me much,
The secret I'll tell to you.

2. "This looks like salad, my dear," said I,
"T'is celery surely I see,
And mayonnaise yellow and thick and rich,
What may this rare flavor be."

3. "A firm spicy apple," she said with a smile,
"Cut into pieces like dice—
I used equal parts, with celery white,
And my salad was made in a trice."

CABBAGE SALAD.
MRS. SMYTHE.

Cut a cabbage into fine pieces. Place in water for a couple of hours with one onion sliced thin. Throw water off, pass through colander. Cover it with the dressing and let it stand for five or six hours. A couple of beets can be chopped up finely and placed with it; this salad will keep for a couple of days.

SALAD DRESSING.

One cup cream, one table spoon sugar, one dessert spoon mustard, one half dessert spoon of pepper and salt, one small onion sliced fine, a couple of radishes sliced, two hard boiled eggs. Crush the yolks into the cream, one pinch mint, two tablespoons vinegar. If cream is not thick enough, crush up potatoes and mix with it. Sour cream can be used as well as sweet cream.

CHICKEN SALAD.

MISS STEVENSON.

One cold chicken, one teaspoonful white pepper, one half head celery, one grain cayenne, yolks two eggs, one tablespoonful vinegar, one tablespoonful capers, one head of lettuce, one gill salad oil, one tablespoonful of cream, white of egg beaten to a stiff froth. Cut the chicken into small square pieces and remove the skin. The celery should be well washed and also cut into pieces of a similar size. Put into a bowl the yolks of eggs, drop into this drop by drop, the oil, and beat them together, the mixture should resemble thick cream, add the vinegar. Put the chicken and celery together in a salad bowl and pour over the compound, sprinkle on also pepper and salt and cayenne; mix all thoroughly together with a fork. Arrange the lettuce around the edge of the salad bowl, sprinkle the capers over the top and garnish the centre with tips of celery.

LOBSTER, CHICKEN OR VEAL SALAD.

MRS. A. J. ELLIOT.

Cut up a chicken, (roast or boiled) fine, salt and pepper well, add a large or two small heads of celery and if lobster some beet-root and the white of a hard boiled egg. Crush the yolk with a pinch of salt, half a teaspoon of pepper, a large teaspoon of mustard, two teaspoons of brown sugar, one teaspoon of olive oil or butter melted, one wineglass of vinegar; mix well with a raw egg well beaten, half a pint of sour or sweet cream, and mix with other ingredients: garnish with either salad or parsley. This is excellent.

LETTUCE CHICKEN SALAD.

MRS. DUNCAN LAURIE.

Having skinned a pair of cold chickens, either mince or divide into small threads. Mix with it a little smoked tongue or cold ham, grated rather than chopped. Have ready one or two fine fresh lettuces, washed, drained and cut small. Put the cut lettuce in a bowl, place upon it the minced chicken in a close heap in the centre. For the dressing: the yolks of four eggs well beaten, a teaspoon of white sugar, a little cayenne, no salt: if you have ham or tongue with the chicken two teaspoonfuls of made mustard, two tables of vinegar, and four tables of salad oil. Stir this mixture well, put it into a small saucepan and let boil three minutes (not more), stirring it all the time, then set to cool, when quite cold cover with it thickly the heap of chicken in centre of salad. To ornament it have ready one half dozen hard boiled eggs, which after the shell is peeled off must be thrown directly into a pan of cold water to prevent discoloring. Cut each egg (white and yolk together) lengthways, into four large pieces of equal size and shape, lay the pieces upon the salad all round the heap of chicken in a slanting direction. Have ready also some red cold beet, cut in small cones of equal size, arrange them outside the circle of egg. This salad should be prepared immediately before dinner or supper. The colder it is the better.

SALMON OR LOBSTER SALAD DRESSING.

MRS. ANDREW T. LOVE.

Two eggs, two tablespoons melted butter, one tablespoon mustard, one half cup milk, (with a small pinch baking soda to prevent curdling), one half cup vinegar, salt and pepper. Mix mustard and butter, then eggs well beaten, milk, stir well, add vinegar, boil gently till as thick as cream. Celery chopped up and added gives a nice flavor and crispness. If cooked in a double boiler it is less likely to burn. This does nicely with chicken or lamb.

SOMETHING NICE FOR THE SALAD COURSE OF A LUNCHEON.

MRS. FRANK DUGGAN.

Select round tomatoes of equal size; peel and scoop out the seeds from the stem end. Place the tomatoes on the ice till shortly before serving; then fill with celery that has been chopped fine and mixed with mayonnaise. Arrange the filled tomatoes on lettuce leaves on a flat dish or plate. Garnish the dish further by placing the ends of celery and sprigs of parsley on top of each tomato. Serve with toasted cheese, biscuits, or salted wafers. Be generous with the filling. Use plenty of the mayonnaise and celery and fill tomatoes to the top.

SALAD DRESSING.

MRS. R. STUART.

Two eggs (well beaten), one cup sweet milk, one half cup vinegar (scant) one teaspoon mixed mustard, one tablespoon butter (melted). Pepper and salt to taste, *mix thoroughly*. Set in kettle of boiling water and stir till it thickens, (about four minutes), when ready to use it add two tablespoons cream.

SALAD SANDWICHES.

MRS. J. LAURIE.

For twenty four slices of bread and butter, take two small tomatoes, one small lettuce, one bunch cress, two tablespoons salad oil, one tablespoon of vinegar, pepper and salt. Shred all the salad finely. Mix well with the dressing and put a little on half the bread and butter. Cover with the other half, press together and trim neatly.

SALAD DRESSING WITHOUT OIL.

MRS. GILMOUR.

The yolks of two egg boiled half an hour, one half egg spoon of mustard, one dessert spoon of sugar, pinch of salt, a little pepper. One cup of sour or sweet cream, one dessert spoon of vinegar.

SALAD DRESSING FOR TOMATOES.

MRS. A. J. ELLIOT.

Half a cup of butter, one cup of sweet milk, one cup of vinegar, one tablespoon of salt, two tablespoons of made mustard, a dash of sugar and cayenne, and four eggs. Slice tomatoes and arrange in layers. Garnish dish with either salad or parsley.

METHOD: Scald the milk and melt the butter with it, pour this on the eggs well beaten, add the salt and then the vinegar, this last slowly, and stir all the time. Then cook in a pot in hot water, until as thick as custard, when cold add the mustard.—Prepared mustard is made as follows: two tablespoons mustard, one teaspoon sugar, half a teaspoon salt, enough boiling water to mix. Half this quantity is enough for ordinary use. The above recipe is also good for chicken.

EGGS.

Humpty Dumpty sat on the wall.
Humpty Dumpty had a great fall.
All the king's horses and all the king's men
Could not set Humpty Dumpty back again.

—MOTHER GOOSE.

Try the freshness of eggs by putting them into cold water; those that sink the soonest are the freshest.

Never attempt to boil an egg without watching the time-piece. Put the eggs in boiling water. In three minutes eggs will be boiled soft; in four minutes the white part will be cooked; in ten minutes they will be hard enough for salad.

PRESERVING EGGS.

MRS. FARQUHARSON SMITH.

(Which keeps them from June to June.)

Half a gallon of fresh lime to five gallons of water added by degrees, two and one half gallons the first day, the rest next, then add one half gallon coarse salt, stir two or three times a day for three days, after this drop in four eggs gently. To test the strength of the lime-water drop in an egg that you know to be fresh, and if it floats the lime is too strong, add another gallon or more of water until you find the egg dropping to the bottom.

CURÉE EGGS.

MISS MITCHELL.

Boil six eggs quite hard, then shell and cut them in half; have drawn butter not too thick, flavor with curée powder. Place your eggs on a side dish, pour your curée round and finish with parsley: makes a pretty lunch dish.

POACHED EGGS.

Have nicely cut hot buttered toast, with a little anchovy paste. After poaching your eggs, put them on the toast and sprinkle finely chopped parsley over them. Garnish the dish with parsley.

ANCHOVY EGGS.

MADAME J. T.

Boil three eggs hard, turn in the water for the first two minutes. Let boil for one hour; cut in two, remove the yolks and leave the whites in cold water not to discolor. Pound three anchovies in a mortar with one tablespoon butter, small pinch of pepper, one shake cayenne, one half teaspoon lemon juice and the yolks of the eggs. When pounded smooth put back into the eggs. Sardines can be used instead of the anchovies.

STUFFED EGGS.

MRS. W. CLINT.

Three eggs, one teaspoon of butter, one teaspoon of parsley, two tablespoons minced ham. Boil the eggs for ten minutes; take off the shells, cut lengthwise, take out the yolks, mash them in a basin, add the butter melted, the minced ham and the parsley. Put the mixture into the whites of the eggs. Put the two halves together. Serve on shallow dish with the following white sauce: one tablespoon each of butter, flour, and salt, one cup milk, one saltspoon pepper. Melt the butter add the flour, then the milk (gradually) and pepper and salt.

BAKED OMELET.

MRS. DUNCAN LAURIE.

One cupful boiling milk, beat the yolks of four eggs, add hot milk, and a tablespoonful melted butter, wet three teaspoonfuls flour in a little cold milk add the beaten whites and beat all, salt and pepper to taste. Bake twenty minutes.

CHEESE OMELET.

MRS. HENRY THOMSON.

Three eggs, well beaten, grated cheese the size of an egg, salt, three tablespoons of fresh cream.

OMELET.

MISS M'GEE.

Seven eggs, one cup of milk, one teaspoonful flour, parsley, pepper and salt. Beat the whites and yolks separately, add the milk, pepper, salt, and chopped parsley and the flour dissolved in a little milk, then add the whites, put in the frying pan, leave on top of the stove for three minutes and put in the oven for five minutes.

OMELETTE.

MISS MAUD THOMSON.

The yolks of four beaten eggs, four tablespoons of milk, a pinch of salt: beat the whites of the four eggs as stiff as possible, add to the above, turn into a frying pan, until the mixture sets and then put in the oven until a golden brown.

CHEESE DISHES.

CHEESE STRAWS.
MRS. J. MACNAUGHTON.

Mix one cupful of any good cheese grated with one cupful of flour, one half saltspoonful of salt, a pinch of cayenne pepper and butter the size of an egg. Add enough cold water to enable you to roll thin. Cut in strips and bake five or to ten minutes in a quick oven.

CHEESE SCALLOP.
MISS FRASER.

Soak one cup of dried bread crumbs in fresh milk. Into this beat the yolks of three eggs, add one teaspoon of butter, and half a pound of grated cheese. Strew upon the top sifted bread crumbs, and bake a delicate brown. Whip the whites of the three eggs to a stiff froth; put on top and return to the oven for a few minutes.

THE CHAFING DISH.

A Relish and a Savory.

WELSH RAREBIT.
MISS GRACE M'MILLAN.

Allow for each person one egg, one tablespoonful of grated cheese, one half teaspoonful of butter, one saltspoon of salt, and a few grains of cayenne. Cook like custard until smooth. Spread on toast and serve at once.

WELSH RAREBIT.
MISS BEEMER.

Select richest and best American cheese, (Canadian will do), the milder the better, as melting brings out strength. To make five rarebits take one pound cheese grate and put in the saucepan; add ale (old is best) enough to thin the cheese sufficiently, say about a wine glassful to each rarebit. Place over the fire, stir until it is melted. Have ready a slice of toast for each rarebit (crusts trimmed); put a slice on each plate, and pour cheese enough over each piece to cover it. Serve *at once*.

GOLDEN BUCK

A "Golden Buck" is merely the addition of a poached egg which is put carefully on top of rarebit.

LOBSTER À LA NEWBURG.
MRS. J. G. SCOTT.

Two pounds of lobster, one half cup of cream, two eggs (hard boiled), one tablespoon flour, two tablespoons of Sherry wine, two tablespoons of butter, salt and cayenne pepper to taste. Break the lobster meat into moderately small pieces, mash the yolks of the eggs with a silver spoon and gradually add half the cream. Place the butter in a granite ware saucepan, add the flour, let it cook slowly for one minute and then pour in the balance of the cream and stir until the liquid thickens. Add the first mixture and then the lobster meat and the whites of the eggs sliced, season with cayenne pepper, and salt, add the wine and serve at once.

LOBSTER À LA NEWBURG.
MRS. HARRY LAURIE.

Two tablespoons of butter, one tablespoon of flour, stir until smooth, add one cup of cream, let it heat through, then add one can of lobster. Pepper and salt to taste and one half cup of Sherry or Port wine, if desired; serve at once on squares of toast. Canned chicken or salmon can be done the same way.

OYSTER COCKTAIL.

MISS RITCHIE.

One dessertspoonful tomato sauce, one shake of tabasco, a sprinkle of horse radish, about half a dozen oysters, and the same on top. Serve in small tumblers on a plate with pounded ice around them and with oyster biscuits.

CRUSTINE.

MRS. A. COOK.

Boil the liver of two chickens, (or turkey will do), pound them to a paste with a piece of butter the size of a walnut, a teaspoon of anchovy and a little cayenne. Serve on hot toast. Small anchovies whole, laid on top are an improvement.

PIES.

"Who dare deny the truth, there's poetry in pie."

—LONGFELLOW.

"Ingenuity, good judgment and great care should be used in making all kinds of pastry. Use very cold water, and just as little as possible; roll thin and always from you; prick the bottom crust with a fork to prevent blistering; then brush it well with the white of egg, and sprinkle thick with granulated sugar. This will give you a firm rich crust.

"For all kinds of fruit pies, prepare the bottom crust as above. Stew the fruit and sweeten to taste. If juicy put a good layer of corn-starch on top of the fruit before putting on the top crust. This will prevent the juice from running out, and will form a nice jelly throughout the pie. Be sure you have plenty of incisions in the top crust; then pinch it closely around the edge; sprinkle some granulated sugar on top, and bake in a moderate oven."

COCOANUT CUSTARD PIE.

MR. JOSEPH FLEIG.

(Baker, Grenoble Hotel, N. Y.)

Place on a deep pie plate a thin layer of pie crust, put a good rim on the side and put into this one half cup of dried cocoanut; fill up with a custard made as follows: three eggs, three ounces of sugar beaten together with flavoring of lemon, vanilla or nutmeg, little salt and add one pint of milk. The custard must be three quarters of an inch thick.

LEMON PIE FILLING.

MRS. JAMES LAURIE.

Mix together two cups of white sugar, yolks of three eggs, juice of two lemons, grated rind of half a lemon; put it on the stove to boil and add at once one tea-cup boiling water, stir smooth, then add two tablespoons of corn starch, mixed in a little cold water, and one tablespoon of butter, boil until it custards.

LEMON PIE.

MRS. GEORGE CRESSMAN.

Grate one lemon, put this down to boil with two-thirds of a cup of water for ten minutes, strain through fine sieve, then add one cup sugar, the juice of a lemon and butter half the size of an egg, let boil a few minutes. Mix two teaspoonfuls of corn-starch and yolk of one egg in half cup milk stir in the mixture letting it boil until thick. Beat whites of two eggs into stiff froth for frosting.

LEMON PIE.

MRS. STRANG.

Take two lemons, three eggs, two tablespoonfuls melted butter, eight table-spoonfuls white sugar; squeeze the juice of the lemons and grate the rind of one, stir together the yolks of three eggs and white of one with the sugar, butter, juice and rind, then one (coffee) cup of sweet cream or milk, beat all for a minute or two; have ready a plate lined with paste, into which pour the mixture which will be sufficient for two pies of the ordinary size. Bake till the pastry is done. Meanwhile beat the remaining whites to a stiff froth and stir in four spoonfuls of white sugar. Take the pies from the oven and spread over equal parts upon each and return them quickly to the oven and bake a delicate brown. Take care that the oven be not too hot, or they will brown too quickly and cause the pie to fall when taken out.

PASTRY.

Four tablespoons of butter, ten teaspoons flour, two teaspoons baking powder, one salt spoon salt, enough water to make a very soft paste.

MOCK CHERRY PIE.

MRS. W. W. HENRY.

One cup cranberries cut up, one half cup of raisins chopped, one half cup of cold water, one teaspoonful vanilla, one tablespoonful corn-starch, two-thirds cup sugar, a little salt. This makes one pie.

MINCE MEAT.

MRS. HENRY THOMSON.

One pound of suet, one pound of fresh tongue, one pound apples, one pound sugar, one pound raisins, one pound currants, two nutmegs, a large teaspoon of cinnamon, ditto of cloves and salt, one half pound of candied peel.

PIE PLANT PIE.

MRS. R. M. STOCKING.

One cup sugar, well beaten with yolks of two eggs; add one pint of pie plant, bake with one crust, then spread beaten whites, with tablespoon sugar over top; return to oven a few moments.

RAISIN PIE.

One cup chopped raisins, one half cup chopped apples, four tablespoons vinegar, one tablespoon cornstarch, one cup of boiling water, one cup sugar, pinch of salt, mix together, bake with two crusts.

SOUR CREAM PIE.

One cup thick sour cream, pinch of salt, one egg, one half cup sugar, scant teaspoon of flour, one half cup raisins; beat cream, sugar, and flour together, lay the raisins round on the top; bake with two crusts.

PUMPKIN PIE.

MISS BEEMER.

One coffeecup of mashed pumpkin, reduced to the proper consistency with rich milk and melted butter or cream, one tablespoonful of flour, a small pinch of salt, one teaspoon of ginger, ditto of cinnamon, one-half nutmeg, one-half teaspoon lemon extract, two-thirds cup of sugar, and two eggs.

PASTE.

One third-cup cup of lard, a little salt; mix slightly with one and one-half cups of flour; moisten with very cold water, just enough to hold together, get into shape for your tin as soon as possible. Brush the paste with white of egg. Bake in a hot oven until a rich brown.

PUDDINGS.

"The proof of the pudding lies in the eating."

ALMOND PUDDING
MRS. STOCKING.

One pint of milk, two eggs, two heaping tablespoons of maple sugar, one heaping tablespoon of cornstarch, flavor with almond; cook milk, sugar, and cornstarch in double boiler, adding yolks of eggs when boiling; pour into pudding dish, cover with whites of the eggs, and brown in oven, to be served cold.

APPLE BATTER PUDDING.
MRS. ERNEST F. WURTELE.

Stew the apples in a pie dish, when soft place the following batter on top: one egg, one tablespoon each of sugar and butter, two tablespoonfuls each of milk and flour, one teaspoon of baking powder, bake forty five minutes in a slow oven, serve with cream.

BANANA PUDDING.
MISS J. P. M'GIE.

Two tablespoonfuls of cornstarch wet with cold water, one cup of white sugar and one third of a cup of butter. Stir together in a dish, pour on boiling water to make a thick custard; stir in the well beaten yolks of three eggs, bring to a boil. Slice thin a few ripe bananas, pour the custard over them. Put whipped cream on top or if not cream the whites of the three eggs well beaten with sugar. To be eaten cold.

BREAD PUDDING.
MRS. ARCHIBALD LAURIE.

Sliced bread to fill a pudding bowl; one layer of bread, one layer of fruit with sugar to taste and small lumps of butter. Continue until bowl is full, put a plate on top and steam for at least two hours, more will do no harm. Turn out a few minutes before wanted to let the juice penetrate the bread that was uppermost.

COTTAGE PUDDING.

MRS. W. W. HENRY.

After rubbing together a cupful of sugar and a tablespoon of butter, add two eggs, and after beating the mixture until light, add a cupful of milk; mix well in a sieve a pint of sifted flour and three teaspoons of baking powder, rub through the sieve into the mixture already made, beat quickly and pour the batter into one large pudding dish or two small ones. Sprinkle with sugar, bake in a moderate oven for forty minutes or thirty if there be two. Serve hot with lemon sauce or any sweet sauce.

Lemon Sauce.—Beat two eggs very light, and add one cup of sugar, one tablespoon of melted butter, one small tablespoon of cornstarch, beat all together, then add one cup of boiling water, cook five minutes, boiling all the while. Cook a little longer if set in a basin of hot water, take from the fire, and add juice of lemon.

CHOCOLATE PUDDING.

One quart of milk scalded, two eggs well beaten, add gradually one cup sugar. With the eggs and sugar mix two thirds cup of cornstarch, and three heaping tablespoons grated chocolate dissolved over hot water, stir into the milk until a soft custard, add one teaspoon of vanilla, serve with whipped cream.

CHOCOLATE PUDDING.

MRS. W. J. FRASER.

One quart of milk, one pint of bread crumbs, one tea cup of sugar, three eggs, three tablespoonfuls of chocolate, one half teaspoonful essence of vanilla. Let the milk come to a boil, scald the bread crumbs, when almost cool, beat the yolks of three eggs, add sugar and chocolate, to the bread and milk. Bake one half hour, slow oven. When cool, beat the whites of three eggs and put meringues.

CARAMEL PUDDING.

MRS. RATTRAY.

Take one coffee cup full of brown sugar, put it in a frying pan over a slow fire and burn it, then pour it into one and a half pints of milk in a saucepan and place the latter on the fire to come to a boil, but do not stir it in case the milk should crack. Blend three tablespoonfuls of cornstarch with a little cold milk, and when the milk and sugar boil stir the starch in. Put it in a mould to get cold and eat with whipped cream.

CARAMEL PUDDING.

MRS. W. W. WELCH.

One pint of milk, one pound of brown sugar, one coffee cup of chopped walnuts, two heaping tablespoons of cornstarch, pinch of salt. Put the milk in a double boiler, when boiling put in cornstarch dissolved in a little cold milk; let it cook a few minutes, put in the sugar which has been previously burnt a little, then add the nuts, stir a few minutes, flavor with vanilla, put into a mould, and eat with whipped cream.

COCOANUT SPONGE.

MISS LAMPSON.

Two cups of stale sponge cake crumbs, two cups of milk, one cup of grated cocoanut, yolks of two eggs and whites of four, one cup of white sugar, one table-spoonful of rose water, a little nutmeg. Scald the milk and beat into this the cake crumbs. When nearly cold add the eggs, sugar, rose water and lastly the cocoanut. Bake three quarters of an hour in a buttered pudding dish. Eat cold, with white sugar sifted over it.

DUTCH APPLE CAKE, LEMON SAUCE.

MRS. STOCKING.

One pint of flour, one half teaspoon salt, one and one half teaspoons baking powder, butter size of an egg; sift flour, salt and baking powder together then rub in the butter thoroughly; beat one egg light with two-thirds of a cup of milk and stir into the dry mixture; spread one half inch thick on a baking pan; pare and core and cut in eight pieces, four apples and stick them into the dough, in rows, and sprinkle over them two tablespoons sugar and bake quickly; serve with sauce as follows: Two cups cold water, ditto of sugar; when it boils, add three teaspoons of cornstarch dissolved in a little cold water; take from fire as soon as it thickens and add one tablespoon of butter and the rind and juice of one lemon, or one teaspoon lemon extract; serve hot.

FRIED CREAM.

MRS. FARQUHARSON SMITH.

Everyone should try this receipt; it will surprise many to know how soft cream could be enveloped in the crust while it is an exceedingly good dish for a dinner course or for lunch or tea. When the pudding is hard, it can be rolled in the egg and bread crumbs. The moment the egg touches the hot lard it hardens and secures the pudding which softens to a creamy substance very delicious. Ingredients, one pint of milk, five ounces of sugar (little more than half a cupful,) butter the size of a hickory nut, yolks of three eggs, two tablespoonfuls of corn starch, and one tablespoonful of flour, (a generous half cupful altogether), stick of cinnamon one inch long, one half teaspoonful of vanilla. Put the cinnamon into the milk and when it is just about to boil, stir in the sugar, cornstarch and flour, the two latter rubbed smooth with two or three tablespoons of extra cold milk: stir it over the fire for fully two minutes, to cook well the starch and flour; take it from the fire, stir in the beaten yolks of the eggs and return it a few minutes to set them; now again taking it from the fire remove the cinnamon, stir in the butter and vanilla and pour it on a buttered platter until one third of an inch high. When cold and stiff cut the pudding into parallelograms, about three inches long and two inches wide: roll them carefully, first in sifted cracker crumbs then in eggs (slightly beaten and sweetened) then again in cracker-crumbs. Dip these into boiling hot lard (a wire basket should be used if convenient) and when of fine color, take them out and place them in the oven for four or five minutes to better soften the pudding. Sprinkle over pulverized sugar and serve immediately.

FEATHER PUDDING.
MRS. W. R. DEAN.

One tablespoon butter, one cup white sugar, two eggs, a little salt, one cup sweet milk, two tablespoons baking powder three cups of flour, one and one half teaspoons flavoring. Steam one hour. Eat with sauce.

FIG PUDDING.
MRS. THOM.

One cup suet, one half pound figs cut fine, two cups bread-crumbs, one cup flour, one half cup brown sugar, one egg, one cup of milk, two teaspoonfuls of baking powder, steam three hours.

GELATINE PUDDING (PINK.)
MRS. W. R. DEAN.

Put one ounce pink gelatine and one quart of milk in a bowl on the stove where it will not get hot; when dissolved add yolks of four eggs, beaten with four tablespoons sugar, stir well, let it just come to the boil, then add the whites well beaten, with four tablespoons of sugar and a dessert spoon vanilla. Turn into a mould and let it cool, then turn out and garnish with whipped cream. This is a very pretty dish.

GRAHAM PUDDING.
MRS. W. W. HENRY.

One and one half cups of graham flour, one cup of milk, one half cup of molasses, one cup chopped raisins, one half teaspoonful salt, one teaspoonful of soda. Sift the graham in order to make it light, but return the bran to the sifted mixture, dissolve the soda in one tablespoon of milk and add the remainder of milk with the molasses and salt, pour this mixture upon the graham and beat well, add the raisins and pour the pudding into a mould. Steam four hours, turn out and serve with sauce.

HONEY COMB PUDDING.
MISS BICKELL.

One cup flour mixed with one cup sugar, one half cup butter and one of milk melted, together, five eggs well beaten; last of all put in two teaspoons soda and one of salt. Steam one hour and a half.

MEDLEY PUDDING.

MRS. THEOPHILUS H. OLIVER.

Three eggs, the weight of three eggs in butter, in sugar, and in flour, beat the butter to a cream. Add the eggs well beaten to the sugar and flour. Put into small teacups. Bake for twenty minutes.

MANITOBA PUDDING.

MRS. STRANG.

Four cups flour, two cups of suet, two cups raisins, one cup currants, two cups sugar (brown), a little baking powder, a little essence of lemon, a little allspice, a chopped apple, a little salt, wet with a small quantity of water, boil four hours.

FOAMING SAUCE.

One half teacup butter, ditto of sugar, beat to a froth, put in a dish and set in a pan of hot water, add one tablespoon of hot water, if liked a little vanilla. Stir one way until it comes to a very light foam.

MARMALADE PUDDING.

MRS. W. R. DEAN.

Two dessertspoons marmalade, two cups bread crumbs, butter size of two walnuts, one half pint of milk, two eggs, two ounces of sugar. Melt the butter and mix with the bread crumbs, marmalade and sugar, add the eggs well beaten and the milk, pour into a well buttered mould, tie a cloth closely over it and boil one and one half hours. Serve with sauce.

CHRISTMAS PLUM PUDDING.

MRS. W. THOM.

One pound each of raisins, currants and suet, three quarters of a pound of bread crumbs, one quarter pound flour, one half pound candied peel, one half pint brandy, one half nutmeg, one quarter pound brown sugar and six eggs. Boil six hours and steam two or three more when required. Caramel sauce. One cup brown sugar, one ounce of butter, and dessertspoon cornstarch, stirred till brown, add boiling water and one wine glass of brandy.

OLD ENGLISH PLUM PUDDING.

MRS. JOHN JACK.

One pound each of stoned raisins, currants, beef kidney suet, granulated sugar, bread crumbs, and flour, one half pound candied lemon and citron peel mixed; one tablespoon salt, one teaspoonful each of finely ground nutmeg, cinnamon and cloves, eight fresh eggs, one half ounce bitter almonds chopped fine, the red part of three large carrots grated, breakfast cupful of strong coffee, strained at breakfast, cupful of molasses, and enough pure apple cider to make the whole of the proper consistency. Mix thoroughly and stand in a warm place over night, put into mould or pudding bag, tie tightly and boil gently for twelve hours. In serving make a sauce of flour, water, butter, and sugar flavored with brandy. Place the pudding on a hot dish, stick a sprig of berried holly in the centre, pour a wineglassful of brandy around it and set fire to it.

ENGLISH PLUM PUDDING.
MRS. BLAIR.

Two pounds and a half raisins, three quarters of currants, two pounds finest moist sugar, two pounds bread crumbs, sixteen eggs, two pounds finely chopped suet, six ounces mixed candied peel, juice and rind of two lemons, one ounce of ground nutmeg, one ounce of cinnamon, half ounce pounded bitter almonds, gill of brandy or if objected to, any flavoring at hand. Stone and cut up the raisins do not *chop* them; wash and dry the currants; cut the candied peel into thin slices; mix all the dry ingredients well together and moisten with the eggs, which should be well beaten; then stir in the flavoring, and when all is thoroughly mixed, add about half a pound of flour and put the pudding into a stout new cloth; or boil in two moulds for twelve hours and serve with rich sauce.

PLUM PUDDING WITHOUT EGGS.
MRS. DAVID BELL.

Two cups of flour, two cups of raisins, two of currants, two cups of suet, one tablespoon sugar, enough water to make a stiff batter, colour with burnt sugar, spice to taste, salt, and lemon peel. *Just before* putting on to boil stir in a couple of tablespoonfuls of raw sago; boil in a cloth, not a shape.

PLUM PUDDING.
MADAME J. T.

Four eggs, yolks and whites beaten together, one half cup brown sugar, one cup molasses, one cup stoned raisins, two cups currants, one cup bread crumbs, two cups chopped suet, three quarters of a nutmeg, grated, the grated rind of a large lemon, one cup flour and one teaspoon baking powder. Steam for three and a half hours in a tightly closed pudding mould well buttered, keeping the water boiling *constantly*. Before serving sprinkle thickly with sugar and pour over this one half cup brandy, and light. Serve with this a sauce made with the juice and rind (grated) of one lemon, put over to boil with one half cup sugar, one half cup water, add one tablespoon cornstarch, one half cup sherry, one half cup brandy. This quantity will serve sixteen people.

PALACE PUDDING.
MRS. SMYTHE.

Two eggs, one cup of flour, one half cup sugar, one quarter cup butter, one teaspoon baking powder, one half teaspoon nutmeg, cream butter, add sugar, eggs, the flour sifted with baking powder, also nutmeg. Grease tin and bake half an hour.

Sauce.—One dessertspoon butter, one dessertspoon of flour, rub well together, add slowly about one cup boiling water, three dessertspoons brown sugar, one teaspoon of molasses. Boil slowly until it thickens and flavor as desired.

QUAY PUDDING.

One cup flour, one half cup sugar, one quarter cup butter one teaspoon soda, one tablespoon jam, two eggs. Cream butter with sugar, add to this the eggs and jam, the flour sifted with the soda. Put into a buttered mould and steam for two hours and serve with lemon sauce.

RAILROAD PUDDING.

MRS. GEORGE ELLIOTT.

Four eggs, beat whites and yolks separately, a cup of sugar to the whites, beat again, then add the yolks, mix a teaspoon of baking powder in a cup of flour and mix the flour and eggs and beat again. Put a sheet of buttered paper in a square pan and bake. When done turn it on a heated towel, the buttered side up and take off the paper and spread with a thick jam or marmalade, roll up quickly and pour sweetened whipped cream over, flavor with vanilla.

RICE PUDDING.

MRS. W. W. HENRY.

One cup of rice boiled soft in water, add a pint of cold milk, and a piece of butter size of an egg, salt to taste, yolks of four eggs, rind of lemon grated. Mix and bake one half hour. Beat the whites of four eggs, stir in a pint of sugar, juice of one good sized lemon. After the pudding is baked and cooled a little pour this over and brown in the oven. Eat cold; this will keep for several days.

SUET PUDDING. (PLAIN.)

MRS STUART OLIVER.

Three quarters of a pound of flour, one quarter of a pound suet chopped fine; mix with an egg and milk.

VICTORIA PUDDING.

MRS. ARCHIBALD LAURIE.

The weight of two eggs in butter, sugar, and flour. Butter and sugar to be beaten to a cream, add the well beaten eggs, two tablespoons of marmalade, then the sifted flour, one half teaspoon soda, dissolved in boiling water. Steam for three hours, not less.

STRAWBERRY SAUCE FOR PLAIN BLANC MANGE.

The whites of two eggs, one cup pulverized sugar, one cup strawberries. Mix all together and whip until stiff.

STRAWBERRY SAUCE FOR PUDDINGS.

MRS. W. W. HENRY.

One cupful of fine granulated sugar, one-half cupful of butter boiled together until it creams, (a wooden spoon best for this), beat the white of an egg until stiff, then add one cup of mashed strawberries, and beat again; add to the mixture, stir well together.

HARD SAUCE.

MRS. GAUDET.

1. One cup of brown sugar, one tablespoon of butter, three drops of vanilla, half a glass of sherry, whipped lightly.

2. One glass of sherry, a tablespoon of molasses, and a tablespoon of sugar.

DESSERTS.

"Custards for supper and an endless host of other such lady-like luxuries." — SHELLEY.

ORANGE FLOAT.
MRS. ERNEST F. WURTELE.

One quart of water, the juice and pulp of two lemons, one coffee cup of sugar. When boiling add four tablespoons of cornstarch; let it boil fifteen minutes stirring all the time, when cold pour over the top of four or five peeled and sliced oranges. Over this spread beaten whites of three eggs. Sweeten and add a few drops of vanilla.

VELVET CREAM.

A large teacupful of white wine, the juice of a nice lemon, one half ounce of isinglass, sugar to taste, let boil together, till nearly all the isinglass is dissolved, then strain and add one pint of cream. Let it stand until nearly cold and then put it into the mould. It requires to be made some hours before it is turned out.

PRUNE JELLY.

Put about three dozen prunes into one quart of boiling water and let them boil for one hour, take out the prunes and stone them making use of half the kernels as a flavoring. Put the prunes back into the water, with the blanched kernels, adding one cup of sugar and let boil half an hour more. Dissolve half a box of Cox's gelatine in water and add to the above and boil ten minutes longer. Put into a mould and serve cold with whipped cream.

FROZEN PUDDING.

Make a custard with three eggs and about one pint of milk, flavor with vanilla and a small cup of white sugar. Put four tablespoons of brown sugar in a frying pan and brown it well. Take from the stove and stir till off the boil, then stir into the custard. Put all in a dipper or deep dish; take a large dish full of snow and coarse salt, put the dipper into this and stir the custard until it is quite thick. Put into a mould and leave in a cool place. Serve with whipped cream.

ARROWROOT WINE JELLY.

Wet two heaping teaspoons of arrowroot with a little cold water, stir it into a cup of boiling water in which has been dissolved 2 teaspoons of white sugar. Stir while it boils ten minutes. Add one tablespoon of brandy, or three of sherry. Put into a mould and serve cold with custard as a sauce. This is very nice for invalids, omitting the sauce.

RICE BLANC MANGE.

One half pound ground rice, one quart of milk, three ounces of sugar, the rind of half a lemon, one half teaspoonful of vanilla. Boil the rice in the milk for twenty minutes with the sugar and rind of lemon, then remove the rind and add the vanilla. Put it into a wet mould.

LEMON JELLY.

MISS CLINT.

Dissolve one package or twelve sheets of gelatine in a little warm water. Then add three and one half pints of boiling water, one pound of sugar and the juice of four lemons. Cool in a mould.

COFFEE JELLY.

MRS. GAUDET.

Two tablespoons of coffee, one package of gelatine, one glass of sherry boiled down to one pint.

ICED APPLES WITH CREAM.

MRS. W. W. WELCH.

Pare and core six apples; cook them in a syrup made of one cup of sugar, and two of water; drop the apples into the boiling syrup; when they are tender put them on a platter, when cool cover with a thin layer of meringue and brown. Let the syrup boil until reduced to one half cupful, when cold, will form a jelly, cut into squares and place over and around the apples. Serve cold with sugar and cream.

FRUIT JELLY.

MISS FRY.

To one large box of gelatine add one half pint cold water. When dissolved add juice of three lemons, two cups sugar, one pint of boiling water. Arrange in layers in a mould. Four bananas and two or more oranges (sliced) six castane nuts chopped fine, six figs, one quarter lb. dates cut into small pieces. Strain jelly over this and cool. Serve with whipped cream. A lining of ladies fingers is an improvement.

COMPOTE OF APPLES.

MISS SEPTIMUS BARROW.

Take five apples, wipe, but do not peel them, take the cores out of four of them and put them in a deep dish. Slice the fifth apple and put the slices and a small lemon sliced with the four apples. One quarter lb. brown sugar to be sprinkled over apples. One half pint of water. Bake until perfectly soft but do not let them lose their shape. Put them in a dish, press and strain the cut up pieces over the cooked apples. To be eaten cold.

POMMES À LA VESUVE.
MISS LAMPSON.

Pile some apple marmalade high in a dish; get ready some macaroni boiled in water well drained, and afterwards sweetened with white sugar, and flavored with brandy; cut it into short lengths, lay it as a bordering round the mountains of marmalade; dust the whole over with powdered sugar, and on the apex form a crater with half a dozen nubs of sugar; pour a gill of brandy over the top, and just before serving set fire to it and place it on the table flaming.

LEMON SPONGE.
MISS BEEMER.

One half box gelatine, juice of three lemons, one pint of cold water, one half pint of hot water, two teacups of sugar, whites of three eggs. Soak one-half box of gelatine in the pint of cold water ten minutes; then dissolve on the fire adding the juice of the lemons with the hot water and sugar. Boil all together two or three minutes; pour into a dish, and let it remain until nearly cold and beginning to set; then add the whites of eggs well beaten and whisk ten minutes. When it becomes the consistency of sponge, wet the inside of cups with the white of eggs, pour in the sponge and set in a cold place. Serve with thin custard, made with the yolks of four eggs, one tablespoonful of cornstarch, one-half teacup of sugar, one pint of milk, teaspoonful of vanilla. Boil until sufficiently thick and serve cold over the sponge. The sponge should be allowed to stand twenty-four hours.

ORANGE SOUFFLÉ.

Pare and slice six oranges, boil one cup sugar, one pint of milk, the yolks of three eggs, one tablespoon of cornstarch. As soon as thick, pour over the oranges; beat the whites of eggs to a stiff froth; sweeten: put on top and brown in oven. Serve cold. Bananas may be used instead of oranges and are far more wholesome from contact with the heat.

GELATINE, WITH FRUIT.

Take one ounce box of gelatine; put to soak in a pint of cold water for an hour. Take the juice of three lemons and one orange, with three cups of sugar; add this to the gelatine, and pour over all three pints of boiling water: let this boil up once, stirring all the time. Take two moulds of the same size, and pour half your jelly into each. Stir into one mould half a cup of candied cherries, and into the other one pound of blanched almonds. The almonds will rise to the top. Let these moulds stand on ice, or in a cool place until thoroughly set, twenty-four hours is best. When ready to serve loosen the sides, and place the almond jelly on top the other, on a fruit platter. Slice down and serve with whipped cream.

EASY ICE CREAM.

One pint of cream, half a pint of milk, teacupful of sugar, two eggs beaten separately, the whites being added last, a teaspoonful of vanilla extract. Stir thoroughly but do not cook, it is quite as nice without. This will be sufficient for six persons. Dissolve half a pound of macaroons in the above mixture before it is frozen and a delicious ice cream may be had.

TRIFLE.

MISS RUTH SCOTT.

One pint of cream well beaten, sugar and flavoring to taste. One quarter of a pound of macaroons which have soaked in sherry for a few minutes. Put in a deep dish alternate layers of macaroons and cream. Preserved cherries and almonds (whole) are a great improvement.

CARAMEL CREAM.

MRS. BENSON BENNETT.

Boil two coffee cups of dark brown sugar, butter the size of an egg and two thirds of a cup of thin sweet cream. Twelve minutes after it commences to boil dissolve half a cup of gelatine in a little cold water, add this to the boiling mixture and nearly a pint of sweet cream all but the two thirds of a cup used in the beginning. Strain and flavor with a tablespoonful of vanilla; pour into a pudding mould and let it stand over night on the ice. Serve with whipped cream.

CLARET JELLY.

MRS. GILMOUR.

One ounce of gelatine, one cup of sugar, the rind and juice of two lemons, two or three pieces of cinnamon, one and one half pints of water, one half pint of claret, one glass of brandy. If Cox's gelatine or Lady Charlotte, is used it will have to be soaked first in a little of the cold water, if the leaf gelatine, boiling water can be poured on it. Put all together into a saucepan with whites of three eggs, put on the fire until it boils and then strain through a flannel bag.

CUP CUSTARD.

MR. JOSEPH FLEIG.

(Baker to Grenoble Hotel, N. Y.)

Five eggs, six ounces of sugar, one quart of milk, extract to flavor, spread cups or moulds with unsalted butter, fill up with the custard, and place in pan filled with one inch water in good oven.

SPANISH CREAM.

MRS. W. R. DEAN.

Yolks of two eggs, two tablespoons sugar, two tablespoons ground rice, one pint of milk. Beat the eggs a little. Put all together on the fire and stir constantly until it thickens. Pour into glass dish and garnish with blanched almonds and strips of citron.

SPANISH CREAM.

MISS GREEN.

Soak one half package of gelatine in one pint of milk for half an hour; while this is soaking take two eggs (separate them) beating the yolks with one half a cup of white sugar, till light, and whip the whites to a stiff froth: when the gelatine is soaked, put the sauce pan on the fire and let gelatine and milk come to the boil: then add the yolks and remove from fire, add the whites and one teaspoon of vanilla. Put in a wet mould and cool.

CHARLOTTE RUSSE.

MISS EDITH HENRY.

To make the jelly for bottom of mould one half a package of gelatine soaked in a little over a tumbler of water, sugar to taste, one half a small cup of cooking wine and enough cochineal to color. Let this stand until stiff. One pint of sweet cream, one half a box of gelatine dissolved, wine to taste, one teaspoon of vanilla, a little over half a cup of sugar: whip cream stiff, then add sugar, wine, vanilla and lastly the gelatine. Beat well together and pour into your mould lined with ladies fingers and jelly.

WINE CREAM.

MRS. W. CRAWFORD.

Two cups of cream, half a cup of sugar, one box of gelatine dissolved in half a cup of sherry over a steamer, when dissolved, strain into cream, and put in a mould and in a cool place.

PINEAPPLE WATER ICE.

MRS. HARRY LAURIE.

Two large juicy pineapples, one and one half pounds of sugar, one quart of water, juice of two lemons. Pare the pineapples, grate them and add the juice of the lemons. Boil the sugar and water together for five minutes. When cold add the pineapple and strain through a sieve. Turn into freezer and freeze.

LEMON WATER ICE.

Four large juicy lemons, one quart of water, one orange, one and one quarter pounds of sugar. Put the sugar and water over to boil. Chip the yellow rind from three lemons and the orange, add to the syrup, boil five minutes and stand away to cool. Square the juice from the orange and lemon add it to the cold syrup, strain it through a cloth and freeze.

ROLLED JELLY.

MRS. W. W. WELCH.

Two eggs, yolks and whites beaten separately. Take the yolks and beat to a cream with one cup of sugar, three tablespoonfuls of milk, then add one cup of flour, one heaping teaspoon of baking powder and the well beaten whites last, also extract as fancied. When baked place on a wet cloth and trim outside edges, cover with preserves, roll in the cloth and let it stand for ten minutes, eat with whipped cream.

JUNKET.

MRS. STUART OLIVER.

Slightly warm one quart milk, add junket tablet dissolved, and two or three tablespoonfuls sugar. Keep in a warm place near fire till solid. Then remove to a cool place till served. Serve with cream and maple sugar or preserves.

CAKES.

"With weights and measures just and true,
Oven of even heat,
Well buttered tins and quiet nerves,
Success will be complete."

"In making cake, the ingredients should be of the first quality—the flour super-fine, and always sifted; the butter fresh and sweet and not too much salted. Coffee A, or granulated sugar is best for cakes. Much care should be taken in breaking and separating the eggs, and equal care taken as regards their freshness. Break each egg separately in a teacup; then into the vessels in which they are to be beaten. Never use an egg when the white is the least discolored. Before beating the whites remove every particle of yolk. If any is allowed to remain, it will prevent them becoming as stiff and dry as required. Deep earthen bowls are best for mixing cake, and a wooden spoon or paddle is best for beating batter. Before commencing to make your cake, see that all the ingredients required are at hand. By so doing the work may be done in much less time.

"The lightness of a cake depends not only upon the making, but the baking also. It is highly important to exercise judgment respecting the heat of the oven, which must be regulated according to the cake you bake, and the stove you use. Solid cake requires sufficient heat to cause it to rise and brown nicely without scorching. If it should brown too fast cover with thick brown paper. All light cakes require quick heat and are not good if baked in a cool oven. Those having molasses as an ingredient scorch more quickly, consequently should be baked in a moderate oven. Every cook should use her own judgment, and by frequent baking she will in a very short time be able to tell by the appearance of either bread or cake whether it is sufficiently done."

SCRIPTURE CAKE.
MRS. STOCKING.

One cup butter	Judges V. 25
Four cups flour	I. Kings IV. 22
Three cups sugar	Jeremiah VI. 20
Two cups raisins	I. Samuel XXX. 12
Two cups figs	I. Samuel XXX. 12
One cup water	Genesis XXIV. 17

One cup almonds . . . . Jeremiah I. 11

Six eggs . . . . Isaiah X. 14

One tablespoon honey . . . . Exodus XVI. 21

One teaspoon cream. . . . . Exodus XII. 19

Baking powder three teaspoonfuls a pinch of salt . . . . Job VI. 6

Spices to taste . . . . I. Kings X. 10

Follow Solomon's advice for making good boys and you will have a good cake.—Proverbs XXIII. 13.

CHRISTMAS FRUIT CAKE.
MRS. THOM.

One pound of flour, one pound of butter beaten to a cream, six eggs beaten separately, two wineglasses of brandy, one pound sugar, one pound of raisins, one pound of currants, one pound of prunes, one pound figs chopped, one half pound mixed candied peel, one half pound almonds, one half teaspoon mixed spice or nutmeg.

FRUITCAKE.

Two pounds of raisins, two pounds of currants, one half pound of citron, one pound of sugar, one pound of flour, eight ounces of butter, ten eggs, two nutmegs, one half ounce of mace, one tablespoon of cloves, same of cinnamon, one glass of brandy, one tablespoon of baking powder, one cup of molasses. Stir butter and sugar together until very light, beat whites and yolks separately and bake in a slow oven.

ORANGE FROSTING.

One pound of frosting sugar, juice of one lemon and one orange, grate rind of orange.

CARAMEL CAKE.

One tablespoon of butter, one cup of sugar, three eggs, one half cup of milk, one and one half cups of flour, two teaspoons of baking powder.

FILLING.—Two cups of sugar, two thirds cup of milk, boil thirteen minutes, add butter the size of a small egg, one good teaspoon of vanilla, when done stir till thick enough to spread and not to run, bake in three, spread between and on top.

CHARLOTTE RUSSE CAKE.
MRS. RICHARD TURNER.

One cup of flour, one cup of sugar, three eggs, two teaspoons baking powder, three tablespoons boiling water. Bake same as sandwich cake.

The filling.—One large cup of cream, one fourth package gelatine, dissolved in a little milk; whip cream to a stiff froth, then add gelatine, sugar, flavoring to taste. Ice the top.

CORNSTARCH CAKE.
MRS. JAMES LAURIE.

One half pound of butter and two cups white sugar stirred together, add the yolks of four eggs, one cup of milk, two cups of cornstarch and one of flour sifted well, one heaping teaspoonful of baking powder and add the whites of the four eggs last. Flavor a little and line tins with buttered paper.

SPONGECAKE. (SPLENDID.)
MRS. ERSKINE SCOTT.

Beat four eggs, over one cup of white sugar, for half an hour, then mix one cup of flour, after it is in the pan pour some essence of lemon on the top and bake immediately.

SPONGE CAKE.
MISS K. H. MARSH.

Beat seven eggs together with their weight in white sugar for half an hour, then sift in the weight of four eggs in flour. Add a little lemon to flavor and bake twenty minutes in a quick oven.

SPONGE CAKE.
MRS. FARQUHARSON SMITH.

Ten eggs; very fresh, one pound fine sugar, the weight of five eggs in flour, the rind of two lemons and juice of one. Break the eggs on the sugar and beat them twenty minutes with two pronged steel carving fork until in a lovely light cream, then grate the lemon rind into it with the juice of one lemon. Sift the flour several times and next mix in the flour most carefully barely stirring to mix it in, if stirred too much it will make the cake heavy. Beat it with the back of the fork towards you. The oven should be a little quick at first until the cake rises, if baking too quickly place a piece of white paper over it and buttered paper should be placed in the pans. N. B.—Delicious if properly made.

SPONGE CAKE.
MRS. ANDREW T. LOVE.

Six eggs, the weight of five in sugar, and three in flour, beat the whites and yolks separately, lemon flavoring.

EASY SPONGE CAKE.

MRS. BLAIR.

Four eggs, two even cups of sugar, three-fourth's cup *hot* water, one and three fourth's cups of flour, even measure, two teaspoonfuls baking powder, salt, flavor with lemon. Beat the eggs separately. To the yolks gradually add the sugar. Mix well. Then add hot water. Mix the baking powder with the flour and add a portion, then part of the well beaten whites, and so on until all is used. Flavor. It will be thin but do not add any more flour, for it is all right. Bake in a moderate oven. It may be baked very thin, cut into shapes like dominos; frost, and mark the lines and dots with a camel's hair brush dipped in chocolate.

CACOUNA CAKE.

MISS K. H. MARSH.

Three cups of sugar, two cups of butter, seven eggs, one pound of raisins, wineglass of wine, one nutmeg, one cup sour milk and one teaspoon soda, five cups of flour. Beat the butter to a cream, then add the sugar and the eggs (well beaten), the fruit, spice and wine, then the flour and lastly the soda dissolved in a cup of sour milk.

DELICIOUS ANGEL'S FOOD.

MISS RITCHIE.

Beat the whites of eleven eggs to a stiff froth, then stir in carefully a cup and a half of sifted granulated sugar, (or better still of castor sugar,) a teaspoonful of vanilla and one cup of flour that has been sifted with a teaspoonful of cream of tartar five times; add this very carefully and mix thoroughly, turn into an ungreased pan and bake in a moderate oven for about fifty-five minutes. When done turn upside down and when cool it will either drop out or it may be easily removed from the pan with a knife.

CHOCOLATE CAKE.

MISS M. A. RITCHIE.

Dissolve two ounces of chocolate in five tablespoonfuls boiling water. Cream half a cup of butter adding gradually one and a half cups of sugar; add the yolks of four eggs, beat thoroughly; then add the chocolate, half a cup of cream or milk, a cup and three quarters of flour, two rounding teaspoonfuls of baking powder, a teaspoonful of vanilla. Beat the whites of the eggs to a stiff froth, stir them carefully into the mixture, and it is ready to bake either in a loaf-pan or in three layer cake pans. Frost with boiled icing flavored with chocolate.

CHOCOLATE CAKE.

MRS. G. CRESSMAN.

One and one half squares of chocolate melted in one half cup of milk, two eggs, reserving white of one egg for frosting, one cup sugar, one teaspoonful soda in one half cup of milk, and one and one quarter cups of flour. Bake in dripping pan. Boiled frosting, one cup of sugar and white of one egg.

MAPLE CREAM CAKE.

One cup of sugar, two eggs, two tablespoonfuls butter, a little less than two cups of flour, two teaspoonfuls baking powder. Bake in two tins. Frosting, one cup and a half of maple sugar, one half cup cream, boil until quite thick then beat until it creams, add the white of one egg, keep beating until thick.

COCOA CAKE.

MISS MAUD THOMSON.

Rub one half cup butter to a cream, with one cup of sugar, add the beaten yolks of two eggs, and beat well. Mix one and one half cups of flour, one teaspoonful baking powder and two teaspoonfuls cocoa, thoroughly beat the whites of eggs stiff, measure one-half cup of milk, and then add a little milk and flour alternately to the egg mixture, lastly add the whites of eggs and one teaspoonful of lemon or vanilla. Bake in a shallow pan about twenty minutes and then frost with plain cocoa frosting.

Icing.—Mix one half teaspoonful cocoa with one cup powdered sugar, add one tablespoonful lemon juice and one tablespoonful boiling water or enough to make the sugar into a paste that settles to a level the moment you stop stirring. Spread at once on the hot cake.

CORN CAKE.

MRS. W. W. HENRY.

One cup of corn meal, one cup of flour, two teaspoons baking powder, sifted with the flour, one egg, two tablespoons melted butter, two tablespoons sugar, little salt, one and one fourth cups of sweet milk, bake in quick oven.

CREWE CAKE.

MISS M. C.

One pound of sugar, one pound of flour, three teaspoons of baking powder, five eggs, one half pound of butter, a little milk, vanilla or lemon flavoring.

CHRISTMAS CAKE.

MRS. GEORGE M. CRAIG.

One cup melted butter, one cup milk, one cup sugar, one cup molasses, six eggs, six cups of flour, two pounds of currants, two pounds raisins, two ounces peel, one teaspoonful of Durkee's baking powder to every cup of flour.

COCOANUT CAKE. (SPLENDID.)

MISS. BEEMER.

Two cups of sugar and one half cup of butter beaten to a cream, slowly add one cup of milk; mix two teaspoonfuls of baking powder with three cups of flour, add this gradually, mixing and then beating, finally the whites of six eggs beaten to a stiff froth and one teaspoonful of lemon extract. This can be made in layers (three) or baked in a square pan.

ICING.

Whites of two eggs, one half pound of cocoanut, and enough powdered sugar to make it sufficiently stiff, one teaspoonful lemon extract.

CREAM CAKE.

MRS. W. R. DEAN.

One cup of butter, one cup of cream or sour milk, two cups of sugar, three cups of flour, four eggs, one teaspoon soda mixed in vinegar and stirred in at the last. Bake in shallow tins.

RAILROAD CAKE.

One tea-cup flour, one ditto of sugar, two teaspoons cream of tartar, one half teaspoon of soda, four eggs. This will form a thick batter. Butter pan and bake about ten minutes.

MOUNTAIN CAKE.

One pound of sugar, one pound of flour, one half pound well beaten butter, one cup sweet milk, six eggs, one teaspoon cream of tartar, one half teaspoon soda dissolved in the milk.

MOUNTAIN CAKE.

MRS. BENSON BENNETT.

Three fourths cup of butter and two cups of sugar beaten to a cream, four eggs beaten very light, three cups of flour with two teaspoonfuls of cream of tartar, one half cup of sweet milk with one teaspoonful of baking soda, bake about twenty-five minutes.

MARBLE CAKE.

MRS. W. R. DEAN.

One cup white sugar, one fourth cup butter, three eggs (whites and yolks beaten separately) one half cup milk, two cups of flour, two teaspoons baking powder. Separate this batter into three parts. In one part put a square of chocolate dissolved in a little hot water, in another part put one teaspoon cochineal to color it. Take a spoonful of each color (white, brown, pink) alternately and bake in long tin pan.

ICING.

White of one egg well beaten, one teaspoon of vanilla, and pulverized sugar.

MARBLE CAKE.

MISS MILDRED POWIS.

(Light Part.)

One fourth cup butter, three fourths cup white sugar, one fourth cup milk, one cup flour, whites of two eggs, one teaspoon of baking powder.

DARK PART.

One fourth cup butter, one half cup brown sugar, one fourth cup molasses, one fourth cup milk, one and one fourth cups of flour, yolks of two eggs, one good teaspoon baking powder, one half a teaspoon (good) each of cloves, cinnamon, nutmeg and mace. Put into the pan a spoonful at a time of each part.

MACAROON TART.

MR. JOSEPH FLEIG.

(Baker, Grenoble Hotel, N. Y.)

Make a paste of three quarters of a pound flour, five ounces of sugar, one half pound butter and two eggs. Roll part of this out to one fourth inch thick layer and spread over a round shallow cake pan about one half inch deep. Bake very slightly. When cold spread with thin layer of jam or jelly, then put with bag and star tube, stripes of macaroon over and bake in a slow oven nice and brown. Put some icing between the stripes after tart is baked.

PASTE FOR MACAROONS AND MACAROON TART.

Take one pound Hoide's Almond paste and mix fine with one pound powdered sugar then add gradually the whites of about eight eggs until the paste gets smooth and soft enough to pass through the bag and tube. For macaroons make paste softer and use round tube or teaspoon. Bake on paper in slow oven.

BUCKEYE CAKE.

MRS. POLLEY.

Two cups sugar, two thirds cup of butter, three eggs beaten separately, one cup of sweet milk, two teaspoons of baking powder sifted with three cups of flour, one teaspoon extract of lemon.

HARRISON CAKE.

One cup of sugar, one cup of butter, four eggs well beaten, one cup molasses, one pound stoned raisins, one teaspoonful each of saleratus, cloves, cinnamon and allspice, one nutmeg and four cups of flour.

ORANGE CAKE.
MRS. A. J. ELLIOTT.

Two cups of flour, one scant cup of milk, one cup of sugar, half a cup of butter, two eggs, one teaspoon soda and two of cream of tartar. Divided in six parts and spread as thin as possible in pans of uniform size. Bake about three minutes: when done lay together with layers of orange filling between. Method: cream sugar and butter together, then add milk in which the soda and cream of tartar has been dissolved, then the eggs well beaten and lastly the flour into which drop a pinch of salt. Beat well and don't scrimp the butter.

ORANGE FILLING.—The juice and part of the grated rind of two oranges, then add one cup of sugar. One tablespoon of flour dissolved in cup of water which is gradually added, then beat the yolk of the egg well, and mix well together, and boil in a steamer until it is as thick as custard or boil about three quarters of an hour. The steamer is the safest as the flour is liable to stick to the pan otherwise.

ORANGE CAKE.
MISS FRY.

Two cups of flour, one cup of sugar, one half cup milk, two teaspoons baking powder, one tablespoon butter, one tablespoon orange juice, two eggs. Beat eggs and sugar, add butter (melted), orange juice and rind of one orange, then milk. Add flour and powder and bake one half hour. Filling:—juice and rind of one orange, one tablespoon each of lemon juice and cornstarch, two tablespoons sugar, one teaspoon butter, one egg. Put orange juice rind, and lemon juice into a cup, then fill with cold water. When it boils, add cornstarch with cold water. Beat yolk of egg with sugar, add this, then butter. When cold spread between layers. Icing. Beat whites of two eggs, add three fourths cup powdered sugar.

LADY CAKE.
MRS. GEORGE LAWRENCE.

One half cup butter, one and one half cups granulated sugar, one cup lukewarm water, two and one half cups of sifted flour, four eggs, whites only, one lemon juice and grated rind, two teaspoons of vanilla extract, two teaspoons of baking powder. Cream the butter in an earthen dish with silver spoon, stirring till light cream color, add sugar beating thoroughly. Sift the flour, add one half of it and the cup of water a little of each, till cup is finished. Beat whites of eggs stiff and dry, add one half, beat, then the rest of the flour. Beat well, add the juice, and grated rind of lemon or vanilla as preferred, next the baking powder and the balance of the beaten eggs. Turn quickly into a deep, well buttered tin, and bake for three quarters of an hour. The tin should be ready for use immediately the baking powder is added. When cold, frost with white icing.

LEMON CAKE.
MISS BEEMER.

One half cup of butter creamed well with one and a half cups of sugar, stir in the yolks of three eggs and one cup of milk; two teaspoonfuls of baking powder sifted with three cups of flour and added alternately with the whites of the three eggs beaten to a stiff froth. Bake in rather a quick oven in three tins of uniform size, and place, between layers, a frosting made of the grated rind of one, and juice of two lemons, and three fourths cup of sugar. Let boil and throw it over the well beaten whites of two eggs. This cake is one that keeps well for five or six days.

NUT CAKE.
MRS. GEORGE M. CRAIG.

One cup sugar, half a cup of butter whipped to a cream with sugar, four eggs, one tablespoonful of milk if needed, quarter of pound of almond nuts chopped fine, two ounces lemon peel, two teaspoonfuls of baking powder and one cup of flour.

NEW PORT CAKE.
MRS. THEOPHILUS OLIVER.

Two eggs, one half cup of white sugar, one half cup of butter, (melted) one quart of flour, two teaspoonfuls of cream of tartar, one cup sweet milk, one teaspoonful of soda dissolved in hot water. Bake in a deep pan (eaten hot).

PLAIN CAKE.
MRS. GILMOUR.

One half cup butter, one cup sugar, three eggs, two cups of flour, two and one half teaspoons baking powder, one cup of milk.

SANDWICH CAKE.
MRS. FRANK LAURIE.

Four eggs, one cup sugar, one cup flour, one teaspoonful of baking powder; mix the yolks and the sugar together, then whip up the whites, mix in with the yolks and sugar, then add the flour and the baking powder putting the latter into the flour. Bake in a hot oven.

SANDWICH CAKE.
MISS M. SAMPSON.

Two thirds cup sugar, one egg, two thirds cup milk, butter the size of an egg, one and one half cupfuls of flour, two teaspoonfuls baking powder. Bake in a quick oven.

SPANISH BUN.
MRS. THOM.

One and one half cups sugar, four eggs, leave out the whites of three for icing, three fourths cup butter, one cup milk, one tablespoonful cinnamon, one teaspoon ginger, one half nutmeg, two cups flour, three spoonfuls baking powder. Bake in flat tin well greased.

ICING.

Take the whites of three eggs, beat to a stiff froth then add a cup of light brown sugar; while the cake is hot, spread this over, return to the oven and brown.

WHITE CAKE. (DELICIOUS.)

MRS. STOCKING.

One cup sugar, one half cup butter, whites of two eggs, one cup of milk or water, two cups of flour, two teaspoons baking powder, cream the butter, stir in sugar, then add milk or water, beaten whites, flour, and lastly the extract.

NUT FILLING.—One cup milk, one cup nut meats, one tablespoon flour, one egg, one half cup sugar, salt. Heat milk sugar and nuts, add egg and flour stirred together; cook until thick.

WALNUT CAKE.

MRS. PEIFFER.

Cream one cup granulated sugar and one fourth of butter, and two eggs, then two heaping cups flour, two heaping teaspoons baking powder sifted four times: while your flour is still heaped in the mixing bowl on top of the butter, etc., add one heaping saucer chopped walnuts, then use as much as you need of one cup sweet milk to make a nice stiff batter, not too thin.

ICINGS FOR CAKES.

APPLE FILLING FOR CAKE.
MRS. W. W. HENRY.

One apple grated, one cup of sugar, one teaspoonful of vanilla, the white of one egg beaten stiff.

CHOCOLATE FROSTING.
MISS MAUD THOMSON.

White of one egg, eight tablespoons powdered sugar, one inch square of chocolate, one half teaspoon vanilla. Do not whip the egg but stir the sugar into it beating until smooth. Place the chocolate in a teacup, float the latter in a saucepan full of boiling water. Cover the pan and when the chocolate melts stir into the frosting and add vanilla and spread upon the cake.

CHOCOLATE ICING (ORIGINAL).
MRS. E. A. PFEIFFER.

One cup granulated sugar, two squares of chocolate, boil till thick (do not stir) then turn into beaten white of one egg.

BOILED ICING.

One cup granulated sugar, boiled till it threads, then turned into the beaten whites of two eggs, and whip till cold.

CHOCOLATE PASTE.
MRS. BENSON BENNETT.

Melt two ounces Baker's chocolate, add one tablespoonful of water, and three of milk, one piece of butter, one egg well beaten, one cup of sugar, make as in lemon marmalade.

FIG CAKE FILLING.
MRS. STOCKING.

One pound figs, one half cup sugar, two thirds cup of water. Boil figs after being chopped fine with sugar and water until thick.

MAPLE SYRUP ICING.

MISS M. W. HOME.

One cup maple syrup, boil until it will harden slightly when dropped in cold water, then pour on the stiffly beaten white of an egg and stir constantly until it thickens, then spread on cake.

MAPLE SUGAR ICING.

MRS. ALBERT CLINT.

One cup of maple sugar, six teaspoonsful water, boiled till thick. White of one egg beaten crisp to be stirred in with the syrup until cool, then spread on the cake. Stir quickly when mixing the syrup and egg.

ORANGE JELLY ICING.

Two oranges, one lemon, one cup of sugar, one cup of water, one tablespoonful of cornstarch. Grate the rinds, add the juice of oranges and lemon; mix the cornstarch with a little water, put in a saucepan and let it come to the boil until thick and clear, stir constantly. When cool enough spread between cakes.

SOFT ICING FOR CAKES.

Two cups of white sugar (teacups), three fourths cup of sweet milk, one half a tablespoonful of washed butter. Boil for ten minutes, take off and stir constantly till it begins to thicken, then spread immediately over cakes. Put in flavoring to taste when you begin to stir.

CREAM ICING.

MRS. RATTRAY.

Take a piece of butter about one half the size of an almond, wash thoroughly to remove salt, beat it to a cream with one tablespoonful of rich cream, flavor with a few drops of lemon, vanilla or any flavoring preferred, then thicken with powdered sugar and spread on cake with a knife dipped in cold water. Let stand before using an hour or longer.

GINGERBREAD AND SMALL CAKES.

GINGERBREAD.
MRS. FARQUHARSON SMITH.

Three fourths pound of butter, two cups of milk, five cups of flour, two cups of molasses, two cups of sugar, five eggs, four tablespoons of ginger. Mix butter and sugar together. Mix the molasses and milk and flour, then the eggs, whip the latter well but not separately, the risings put in last, one teaspoonful of baking soda, and two of cream tartar; if sour milk or cream is used the latter need not be used; a large flat pan with well buttered paper. Cooked in a moderate oven it takes about three quarters of an hour to bake. Sour cream makes it much richer and not quite so much butter required.

SPONGE GINGERCAKE.
MRS. ANDREW T. LOVE.

Four eggs, three cups molasses, one cup sugar, one half cup of milk or water, one half cup butter, three small tablespoons ginger, one half teaspoon nutmeg, cloves, cinnamon, one and one half pounds flour light weight, three teaspoon baking powder, lemon or vanilla flavoring.

SOFT GINGERBREAD.
MRS. W. R. DEAN.

One quart of flour, rub in it one half cup butter, one pint of molasses, two eggs, one tablespoon ginger, two teaspoons soda dissolved in a tumbler of milk. About forty minutes to bake.

SOFT GINGERBREAD.
MISS BEEMER.

Two cups molasses, one half cup of shortening (lard), three fourths cup boiling water, one tablespoon each of ginger, cinnamon and saleratus, (soda) two table-spoonfuls vinegar, three and one half cups of flour, one teaspoon salt (even), melt the molasses and shortening on the stove slowly, mix the saleratus with the boiling water and add it to the above, then add the vinegar; mix the ginger, cinnamon and salt with the flour and stir in slowly. Bake in a long flat tin in a moderate oven about half an hour.

COOKIES.

MRS. W. H. POLLEY.

Three eggs, three cups sugar, one and one half cups of butter, one half cup sweet milk, one teaspoonful saleratus, one tablespoonful of caraway seeds and enough flour to roll out.

MOLASSES COOKIES.

One cup molasses boiled, one half cup lard, one half cup of butter, one teaspoonful each of ginger and saleratus, flour enough to roll out.

OATMEAL COOKIES.

MRS. WADDLE.

One cup hot water, one cup butter and lard mixed, one cup of sugar, two cups of oatmeal, two cups of flour, one teaspoon soda in a little boiling water, roll thin and bake in a hot oven.

COOKIES. (SPLENDID).

MRS. FRANK GLASS.

One cup sugar, one cup butter, two eggs, three teaspoons baking powder, one tablespoon water, flour to roll, one teaspoon vanilla, roll out but a little of the dough at a time.

GINGER SNAPS.

One and one half cups molasses, one cup brown sugar, pinch of ginger, one teaspoon soda, one half cup sour milk, one half cup of butter, one half cup lard, flour to roll.

DOUGHNUTS.

One half cup butter and one cup sugar beaten together, three eggs beaten light, one half cup sour milk, one teaspoon soda, flour enough to roll fry in hot lard.

FRIED CAKES.

MRS. HENRY THOMSON.

One cup sugar, butter size of an egg, one cup milk, two eggs, one quart of flour, two teaspoons cream of tartar, one half teaspoon of soda, spice to taste.

CRULLERS.

MRS. ARCHIBALD LAURIE.

One cup sour cream, two eggs beaten separately, three fourths of a cup sugar, one half teaspoon soda dissolved in boiling water, one teaspoon cream of tartar sifted with flour, flour enough to roll rather soft, and boil in fresh lard.

CRULLERS.
MISS GREEN.

One pint of cream, four eggs, one cup of sugar, three teaspoonfuls of baking powder, flour enough to make a batter fit for rolling.

CROQUIGNOLES.
MADAME A. GRENIER.

One half pint of cream, one half pint of milk, four eggs well beaten, three quarters of a pound of granulated sugar, one quarter of a pound of butter blended with the flour, one teaspoon of soda dissolved in vinegar, two teaspoonfuls of baking powder, flour enough to roll out.

CROQUIGNOLES.
MRS. ARCHIE COOK.

Three eggs, one cup of milk, one quarter of a pound of butter, one and one half cups of sugar, three teaspoons of baking powder, flour enough to roll out and a little essence of lemon.

DOUGHNUTS.
MR. JOSEPH FLEIG.
(Baker, Grenoble Hotel, N. Y.)

One half pound sugar, three oz. butter, four eggs, one pint of milk, a little essence of lemon and two pounds of flour with one ounce of baking powder.

WAFER JUMBLES.

One half pound sugar, one half pound butter and one half pound flour, three eggs and vanilla flavoring. Place on a long flat pan using bag and tube, bake in good oven.

PUFFETS. (HOT TEA CAKE.)
MRS. BENSON BENNETT.

One and one half pints of flour, three eggs, one half cup of butter, one half cup of powdered sugar, two teaspoonfuls of cream of tartar, one ditto of carbonate of soda, one half pint of milk.

BOSTON CREAM CAKE.
MRS. JOHN MACNAUGHTON.

Boil one quarter pound butter in one half pint of water. Stir in while boiling six ounces of flour. Take from the fire and stir in gradually (when it has cooled a few minutes) five eggs well beaten. Add one quarter teaspoon soda and a little salt. Above recipe makes about two dozens cakes. They must be baked from twenty minutes to half an hour. Be sure to let them bake enough. Do not think them burning unless you see them doing so.

CREAM FOR FILLING.

Boil three quarters of a pint of milk, and stir in while boiling two eggs, one cup of sugar, and one half a cup of flour beaten together very smoothly. Flavor to taste, and when cool fill the cake through a small slit made in the side of each with a sharp knife. The cakes must also be cool before they are filled.

DOMINO CAKES.

Mix together as quickly as possible two cupfuls of sugar with one of butter, then the beaten yolks and lastly the stiffly whipped whites of three eggs, and a teaspoonful extract of lemon. Mix in just enough flour to roll the mass out very thin and cut it into domino shape. After the cakes are in the pan, brush with the white of an egg, using a feather, and sprinkle them with comfits. Bake a light brown. These are delicious and pretty, and will keep fresh a long time.

QUEEN CAKES.

MRS. SMYTHE.

One cup of flour, four tablespoons of sugar, two tablespoons butter, one half teaspoon baking powder, ditto of lemon extract, two eggs and a few currants. Beat eggs with sugar, add butter melted, then the flour and essence of lemon, sprinkle a few currants at the bottom of small moulds. Bake about fifteen minutes.

SHREWSBURY CAKES.

MISS HENRY.

Rub to a cream six ounces of sugar, with six ounces of butter, add two well beaten eggs and work in twelve ounces flour, adding a teaspoonful of rose water. Roll out thin and cut into small cakes.

CONFECTIONS.

"Sweet meats, messengers of strong prevailment in an unhardened youth." — SHAKESPEARE.

SALTED ALMONDS.
MRS. BENSON BENNETT.

Blanch, put into a baking pan, and to each pound allow a tablespoonful of butter, stand them in the oven, watch and shake until all are nicely browned; take out and lift carefully from the grease, dust thickly with salt, and put in a cool place at once.

BUTTER SCOTCH. (ORIGINAL.)
MRS. E. A. PFEIFFER.

One pint of maple syrup, butter size of an egg, boil till stiff when dropped in cold water.

CHOCOLATE CREAMS.
MRS. EDWARD C. POWERS.

Two pounds confectioner's sugar, one fourth pound grated cocoa-nut, one tablespoonful vanilla, a pinch of salt, whites of three eggs (beaten very stiff); mix all together, and roll into small balls; let stand one-half hour; then dip into the chocolate prepared thus: One half cake Baker's chocolate (grated fine), two tablespoonfuls butter. Warm the butter; mix in the chocolate. When cool dip the creams in, and set on a buttered plate to harden.

VANILLA TAFFY.

Three cups of granulated sugar, one cup of cold water, three tablespoonfuls of vinegar. Cook without stirring until it threads; add one tablespoonful of vanilla; let cool; pull until white; cut into small squares.

EVERTON TOFFEE.
MRS. FRANK LAURIE.

Put one pound of brown sugar, a breakfast cupful of cold water, eight ounces of unsalted butter, mix well together in a small preserving pan, stir till quite through the boil. Test the strength of the toffee as you do barley sugar.

BUTTER SCOTCH.

MRS. W. R. DEAN.

Two cups brown sugar, one tablespoon water, butter size of an egg. Boil *without stirring*. Try it in cold water, and it is done when it hardens on the spoon. (Add one teaspoon vanilla if preferred). Pour on buttered plates. Mark into squares before it hardens, and when it is cool it will break off neatly.

CHOCOLATE FUDGE.

Four cups sugar (white), two cups milk, one pound butter, one cup grated chocolate, vanilla to taste. Nuts may be added. Boil and beat thoroughly (as for sucre à la crême) pour on buttered plates and cut into squares.

NUT CANDY.

Two cups white granulated sugar, one half cup sweet milk. Boil for *about* ten minutes, and add three quarters cup cut up walnuts. Remove from stove and beat thoroughly and when it thickens pour out on buttered plates. Cocoanut candy may be made same way. If the candy does not thicken after being beaten, it is not boiled sufficiently and can be put back on stove. Stir constantly through, if the *nuts* are in.

PICKLES.

"Peter Piper picked a peck of pickled peppers." — MOTHER GOOSE.

CANADIAN TOMATO CHUTNEY. (SPLENDID.)
MRS. RATTRAY.

One peck green tomatoes, twelve large red onions, one large cauliflower, two heads celery, two heads garlic, six red peppers. Wash tomatoes and dry them; peel the onions, cut the cauliflower into small pieces, also the celery and peppers and scald and separate the garlic. When all are prepared slice the tomatoes and onions, and put a deep layer into your preserving pan mixing some of the other ingredients with them, then sprinkle with coarse salt, and continue layer by layer until all are in the pan. Let this stand twenty-four hours, then drain the liquor off and add the following, placing all on the fire to boil at least two hours, or until soft; three pints of vinegar, three pounds brown sugar, one tablespoonful of cloves (ground), and ditto of cinnamon, allspice and pepper, one ounce of turmeric powder. Stir all from the bottom frequently lest it should stick and scorch.

TOMATO CHUTNEY.
MRS. J. MACNAUGHTON.

Slice one peck of green tomatoes into a jar, sprinkle a little salt over each layer and let stand for twenty-four hours, drain off the liquor; put the tomatoes into a kettle with a teaspoonful each of the following spices: ground ginger, allspice, cloves, mace, cinnamon, a teaspoonful of scraped horse-radish, twelve small or three large red peppers, three onions, a cup full of brown sugar, cover all with vinegar; boil slowly for three hours.

CRAB APPLE PICKLE.
MRS. J. MACNAUGHTON.

One quart good vinegar, six cups brown or maple sugar, one teaspoonful each cloves, cinnamon and allspice. Boil vinegar and sugar together, skim and add spices. Take the blossom end from the apples and put as many in at a time as will lie on the top of the vinegar without crowding and cook until easily pierced with a straw. Seal in glass fruit jars.

CHILI SAUCE.

MRS. WADDLE.

Six large tomatoes, three small green peppers, one onion, two large table-spoons sugar, salt to taste, one and one half cups vinegar, tomatoes peeled, peppers and onions chopped fine and all boiled one hour.

CHOW CHOW.

MRS. SEPTIMUS BARROW.

One peck green tomatoes chopped fine, one dozen good large onions chopped fine, two quarts vinegar, two pounds brown sugar, one tablespoon each of allspice and cloves, two tablespoons each of ground mustard, black pepper and salt, one half teacup grated horse-radish. Mix all together and stew until perfectly tender, stirring often to prevent burning. Seal in glass jars while hot.

CHOW CHOW. (ORIGINAL.)

MRS. E. A. PFEIFFER.

Two gallon tomatoes, twelve onions, two quarts vinegar (malt), one quart of sugar (brown), two tablespoons of coarse salt, ditto of mustard, and black pepper, one tablespoon of allspice and ditto of cloves.

CELERY SAUCE.

MRS. THEOPHILUS OLIVER.

Fifteen ripe tomatoes, two peppers, five large onions, seven and a half table-spoonfuls of white sugar, two and one half tablespoonfuls of salt, three cups of vinegar, two heads of celery, chop celery onions, and peppers, and boil all together an hour and a half.

MUSTARD PICKLE.

MRS. J. MACNAUGHTON.

Six ounces ground mustard, two ounces corn starch, one and one half ounces of turmeric, one ounce curry powder, two quarts white wine vinegar. Mix the ingredients in cold vinegar and stir into the rest of the vinegar when boiling. Stir half an hour and pour over the pickles which have been covered with a strong brine of salt and boiled for three minutes, then strained and put in bottles or jars. This is nice for cauliflower and is sufficient for one large head which must be cut into small pieces. Other vegetables such as gherkins may be used.

PICKLE FOR CORN BEEF.

MRS. HENRY THOMSON.

Two gallons of water (soft the best), two and one half pounds salt, one half pound sugar, two ounces of salt petre.

PICKLED PEACHES.
MISS EDITH HENRY.

Eight pounds of peaches, four pounds of white sugar, one quart of vinegar, one ounce of cinnamon, one ounce of cloves. Select large firm freestone peaches, remove the skins and put into a jar. Put the sugar, vinegar, and spices into a kettle, let it come to a boil, skim, and pour over the fruit. The next day pour off the syrup and boil again and pour over the peaches. Then the third day, put the fruit and all into the kettle and boil until tender, or about ten minutes. If you use ground spices put in cheese cloth bag.

SWEET TOMATO PICKLE.
MRS. JOHN JACK.

One peck of green tomatoes sliced, six large onions sliced, strew a teacupful of salt over them, let them remain over night, drain off in the morning, then take two quarts of water and one of vinegar, boil them in it fifteen or twenty minutes, put them in a sieve to drain, then take four quarts vinegar, two pounds brown sugar, half pound white mustard seed, two tablespoonfuls ground allspice, same of cloves, cinnamon, ginger, and mustard and one teaspoonful cayenne pepper. Put all in a kettle and cook fifteen minutes slowly. Follow directions, and you will pronounce them capital.

TOMATO CATSUP.
MISS GREEN.

One peck of ripe tomatoes, one quart onions in an enamel kettle: boil till soft, mash and strain through a coarse sieve. One quart or more vinegar and from two to three tablespoons of salt, one ounce of mace and one tablespoon each of black pepper, cayenne pepper, and ground cloves, one and one half pounds brown sugar. Mix and boil slowly for two hours. Bottle and seal.

PRESERVES.

"Will't please your honor taste of these conserves."

—SHAKESPEARE.

CANNING FRUIT.
MISS M. SAMPSON.

To can strawberries, raspberries or plums: to each pound of sugar add one half pint of water, boil till you have a rich syrup, let stand till cold; have your jars packed full of raw fruit (not crushed) and fill with the cold syrup, put on the covers and screws, (not the rubber rings,) and place in cold water up to the neck of the jars, you will need straw or chips between the jars to prevent them touching each other or burning on the bottom, let the water boil for fifteen minutes, have some hot syrup to fill jars, put on rubber rings, screw up tightly and keep in a cool dark place.

CANNED FRUIT JUICES.
MRS. FARQUHARSON SMITH.

Fruit juice may be kept for a long time by canning the same as whole fruit. They are convenient for water ices and summer beverages. Mash the fruit and rub the pulp through a fine sieve. Mix about three pounds of sugar with one quart of fruit juice and pulp. Fill Mason's jars with the syrup, cover and place in a heater with cold water to cover nearly to the top of the jar. Let the water boil half an hour, then fill each jar to the brim, seal and cool in the water.

TO BRANDY PEACHES.

To three pounds of sugar add a pint and a half water; boil and skim it; prepare eight pounds of ripe clingstone peaches: wash and rub with a coarse towel until all the down is off, then pierce them with a fork and throw them into the syrup and boil them until a sharp straw can punctuate them: as they soften put them into your jar, which must be kept closely covered. Boil your syrup until it thickens, while hot, add a quart of the best brandy and throw it over your peaches, tie the jar down closely.

CURRANT JELLY.

Currants should not be over ripe. Equal parts of red and white currants or currants and raspberries make a delicately colored and flavored jelly. Pick over and remove the leaves and poor fruit, and if filthy wash and drain them but do not stem them. Mash them in a porcelain kettle, with wooden pestle without heating as that makes the jelly dark. Let them drain in a flannel bag over night. *Do not* squeeze them, or the jelly will be cloudy. In the morning measure a bowl of sugar for each bowl of juice, and heat the sugar carefully in an earthern dish in the oven. Stir it often to prevent burning: boil the juice twenty minutes and skim thoroughly. Add the hot sugar and boil from three to five minutes or till it thickens on a spoon when exposed to the air. Turn at once into glasses and let them remain in the sun several days then cover with paper dipped in brandy and paste paper over the tops of the glasses. One who is authority on this subject recommends covering with melted paraffine, or putting a lump of paraffine in the jelly while still hot. After draining the juice, the currants may be squeezed and a second quality of jelly made, it may not be clear but will answer for some purposes.

CANDIED PEEL.

MRS. DAVID BELL.

Put the lemon or orange skins, in strong salt and water, when they are soft enough to pass a straw through, take them out and soak them changing the water till all the salt taste is gone, then simmer them in thin brown sugar syrup till clear; take them out, place on a dish, and let them remain for a day or two. Boil the syrup till thick, then fill the skins with it and put away to dry.

LEMON HONEY. (FILLING.)

MRS. FRANK GLASS.

One pound of butter, four pounds of sugar, two dozen eggs leaving out eight whites, rind and juice of one dozen lemons. Put all together, and let simmer until it thickens like honey. Put into jars, can be kept for years.

PUMPKIN JAM.

MRS. HENRY THOMSON.

Peel and seed, then, cut into pieces two or three inches square, lay on a dish to dry till next day, then put into the preserving pan and barely cover with molasses. To a medium sized pumpkin put one ounce cloves and about a dessertspoon of ginger or as much as will taste; let it boil until the pumpkin is quite soft. One half dozen apples (sour) just cored not peeled is a great improvement. The molasses must only come to the top of your pieces, not nearly cover them.

FRUIT JELLY.

MRS. DUNCAN LAURIE.

Dissolve two ounces of tartaric acid in one quart of cold water, pour it on to five pounds of strawberries, currants, or raspberries. Let it stand twenty-four hours. Then strain it without pressing or bruising the fruit. To every pint of clear juice add one and one half pounds of white sugar. Stir frequently till the sugar is dissolved. Then bottle and cork air tight. Keep in a cool, dark place. When required for use dissolve one ounce gelatine in one half pint boiling water, add one and one half pints syrup. Pour in a mould and set away to stiffen. Serve with whipped cream.

GRAPE JELLY.
MRS. GEORGE ELLIOTT.

Mash the grapes in a preserving pan, put them over the fire and cook until thoroughly done. Strain through a jelly bag and to each pint of juice allow one pound of sugar. Boil the juice rapidly for ten minutes, add the sugar made hot in the pan in the oven, and boil rapidly three minutes more. Excellent.

MARMALADE.
MRS. FARQUHARSON SMITH.

Cut the oranges in half and work in a spoon to remove the inside. Slice the peel very fine. Take the skin and seeds from the pulp and mix peel and pulp together and weigh them. For every pound of fruit, pour three pints of cold water over it and let stand twenty four hours. Boil till chips are tender (about an hour and a half). This absorbs a great deal of the fluid. Let it stand another twenty-four hours. To every pound of boiled fruit, put one and one quarter pounds of sugar. Boil till syrup jellies, and chips are transparent. Boil pippins and skins in a gallon of water, and strain.

BITTER ORANGE MARMALADE.
MRS. R. STEWART.

One dozen bitter oranges, three sweet oranges, three lemons. Slice or shave the bitter oranges and lemons *very thin* laying aside the pips in a bowl; pare or slice the sweet oranges. To every pint of fruit add four pints cold water, cover the pips with water, let stand for twenty-four hours, boil till quite tender putting the pips in a muslin bag when ready: to every pound of fruit add one and one half pounds white sugar and boil till it jellies, from twenty to thirty minutes.

CURRANT MARMALADE.
MRS. W. W. HENRY.

Seven pounds of currants, six pounds of sugar, two pounds of raisins, two oranges. Cook one and one half hours. Strain out the juice of currants, seed the raisins, and chop fine. Use all of the orange but the seeds, chop fine.

RHUBARB MARMALADE.
MRS. THEOPHILUS OLIVER.

Peel and cut the rhubarb into small pieces, take the rind of one lemon, cut into chips; to each two pounds of the rhubarb then weigh three quarters of a pound of white sugar to each pound of the fruit. Put the fruit and sugar in a basin in layers and let it stand all night. Pour off the syrup and boil it for twenty minutes, add the fruit and boil for twenty minutes more, when the marmalade should be ready to put in pots.

PRESERVED RAW PINEAPPLE.

MRS. W. COOK.

Pare the pineapples and take out all the eyes. With a sharp knife, cut the pine-apple in thin slices cutting down sides until the heart is reached, this is to be discarded. Weigh the sliced pineapple and put in a large earthen dish. Add to it as many pounds of granulated sugar as there are pounds of fruit and stir well. Pack this mixture in quart or pint jars: cover tightly and put away. The pineapple will keep a year or more and be perfectly tender and fine flavored. It is best to choose fruit not over ripe.

PRESERVED TOMATOES. (ORIGINAL).

MRS. E. A. PFEIFFER.

Take two gallons large smooth green tomatoes, make a pickle of three pints of vinegar, and one quart of water, two tablespoons salt, one tablespoon each, spice, cloves and cinnamon, one pound of sugar: scald spices ten minutes in vinegar and water, then add tomatoes and scald till tender, slice for table, pour sauce over. N. B. Strain spices, over the tomatoes, and seal while warm; some prefer without salt.

TO PRESERVE TOMATOES FOR WINTER USE.

MRS. ERNEST F. WURTELE.

To fifteen pounds tomatoes, put three ounces of white sugar, and three ounces of salt, boil very hard for twenty minutes. Fill up pint jars to overflowing and screw down tight; as they cool off, screw them again so as to be sure they are quite tight. This quantity fills ten pint jars. Skin the tomatoes before boiling, this is quickly done by pouring boiling water over them.

BEVERAGES.

BOSTON CREAM. (A SUMMER DRINK).
MRS. W. FRASER.

Make a syrup of four pounds of white sugar, with four quarts of water; boil; when cold add four ounces of tartaric acid, one and one half ounce of essence of lemon, and the whites of six eggs beaten to a stiff froth; bottle. A wineglass of the cream to a tumbler of water, with sufficient carbonate of soda to make it effervesce.

CLARET CUP.
MRS. HENRY THOMSON.

Six bottles of claret, one of sherry, three wine glasses of brandy, five bottles of soda water, sugar to taste.

GINGER BEER.
MRS. DUNCAN LAURIE.

One quarter pound white ginger, two ounces cream tartar, two pounds white sugar, juice of two lemons, three gallons of hot water; boil one hour, cork while hot.

GINGERETTE.
MRS. ALBERT CLINT.

Four and one half pounds of loaf sugar, one and one half ounce tartaric acid, four ounces tincture of ginger, one ounce essence of capsicum, two drops of cassia. Put the above ingredients into a crock that will hold two gallons of boiling water; one pound of brown sugar to be burnt in a pan till it is the color of coffee, then add to it the other ingredients. The boiling water is the last thing to be poured on the ingredients. Stir until the sugar is dissolved. When cold, bottle, cork tight and put away for use. The burnt sugar gives it a pretty colour.

GINGER CORDIAL.
MRS. ERSKINE SCOTT.

Ten lemons, one gallon of whisky, six ounces of root ginger, (to be bruised) and put with the whiskey on the lemons, after cutting them up in slices, and left for three weeks. Then take five pounds of white sugar, and pour over it three pints of boiling water, and put on the fire until it is melted. When it is cold, pour over the lemons, having first strained them, bottle and cork tight.

GRAPE JUICE.

MRS. GEORGE LAWRENCE.

To ten pounds grapes (Concord), two pounds white sugar, wash grapes, cover them with water in preserving kettle, and boil for thirty minutes, strain through coarse cheese cloth, let cool, add sugar, boil twenty minutes longer, and bottle while *boiling hot*, and cork and seal with sealing wax.

GRAPE WINE.

MRS. E. A. PFEIFFER.

Take fresh blue grapes, stems must be green, mash well, put in preserving pan, and warm, not boiling heat, strain, first through cheese cloth, then through flannel, return to pan, sugar to taste, bring to boiling heat, bottle while hot, cork well and seal. Have kept it over a year without any fermentation. Original.

GRAPE JUICE.

MRS. J. MACNAUGHTON.

Pick over and wash your grapes. Concords are said to be preferable. Put them in your porcelain kettle with just enough water to prevent sticking. When the skins crack remove from fire, pour into a flannel bag, not more than a quart at once, and press out the juice. Add nearly half as much sugar as juice and return to the kettle. When the sugar is all dissolved and the juice boiling, pour into cans and seal. Pint cans are preferable; when opened this can be diluted with water to suit the taste, and will keep perfectly sweet for several days if kept in a cool place.

RASPBERRY ACID.

MRS. GEORGE M. CRAIG.

Dissolve five ounces of tartaric acid in two quarts of water, pour it on twelve pounds of red raspberries in a large bowl, let it stand twenty-four hours, strain it without pressing: to a pint of this liquor, add one and a half pounds of white sugar, stir until dissolved, bottle but do not cork for several days, when it is ready for use two or three tablespoons in a glass of ice water will make a delicious drink.

RASPBERRY VINEGAR.

MRS. STUART OLIVER.

Cover with vinegar and let them stand about a week, stirring every day, then strain the fruit and to each pint add a pound of sugar. Boil till it seems as a syrup about one half an hour, bottle, cork when cold.

LEMON SYRUP.

MRS. THOM.

One pound powdered frosting sugar, one quarter pound tartaric acid, one quarter pound carbonate of soda, forty drops essence of lemon. Add the latter to the sugar, mix well. Having dried it well pass it through a sieve, and keep in a closely corked bottle. A teaspoonful will suffice for a tumbler of water.

LEMON SYRUP.

MRS. FARQUHARSON SMITH.

Two ounces citric acid, one ounce tartaric acid, one half ounce epsom salts, five pounds white sugar. Grate the rind of three lemons, juice of six lemons, three pints boiling water, when cold add the whites of two eggs well beaten, strain through muslin, and then bottle.

LEMON SYRUP.

MRS. ARCHIBALD LAURIE.

One quart juice of fresh lemons, the yellow skin only of six lemons, one quart boiling water, four pounds white sugar. Let it stand for twenty-four hours. If not quite dissolved melt over a gentle heat. Filter through a jelly bag and bottle tightly corked, will keep for three months in a cool place.

COOKING FOR THE SICK.

NOURISHING CREAM FOR CONVALESCENTS.
MRS. BLAIR.

Beat the yolks of four eggs, three tablespoonfuls of sugar, and the rind (grated lightly), and juice of an orange, or lemon. Add a teaspoonful of powdered sugar to the whites of the eggs and beat until stiff. Place the vessel containing the beaten yolks in a pot of boiling water, cook gently, stirring all the time. When it begins to thicken stir in the whites of the eggs until thoroughly mixed, then put it to cool. Serve in small glasses.

BEEF TEA FOR INVALIDS.
MRS. W. COOK.

One pound lean beef and one pound veal, cut up small, and put in a wide mouthed jar. Pour two wineglasses of cold water or wine on it, one teaspoon salt, and a little mace if liked. Cork the jar well and tie a bladder over it. Place the jar in a deep saucepan of cold water which must not be allowed to cover the cork. Let it boil slowly four hours or more and strain through a sieve. One tablespoonful of this is equal to a cup of ordinary beef tea.

CALF'S FOOT JELLY.

Make your stock of calves feet and two ox feet. Add to it if very firm a pint of water, juice of four lemons and rind of two, five eggs, shells and all, whites beaten well, one ounce cinnamon, one ounce cloves, sugar to taste, about one and one half pounds and one bottle of sherry. Put all into the pan and stir well. Let it boil a minute or two and then throw in a cup of cold water, cover closely for ten minutes, skim and run through the bag.

GRUEL.
MRS. SMYTH.

One large cup oatmeal, cover with cold water, stir well and let stand a few minutes. Strain, adding a little more boiling water or half milk, to the water strained. Stir it until it comes to the boil. Cook five minutes or longer. When ready for serving, add a little salt, sugar and nutmeg.

BAKED LEMON FOR A COLD.

MRS. SEPTIMUS BARROW.

Dose a teaspoonful. Bake a lemon till soft, take out all the inside, and mix with as much sugar as it will hold, strain and stand till cold when it will jelly.

BREAD, BUNS, FRITTERS.

BOSTON BROWN BREAD.

MRS. RICHARD TURNER.

One cup Graham flour, one cup corn meal, one cup wheat flour, one large cup raisins, one teaspoon baking soda, one half cup warm water, one pinch of salt. Steam four hours: nice sliced and steamed for breakfast.

BROWN BREAD.

MRS. R. STEWART.

One cup Graham flour, one cup wheat, one cup yellow corn meal, one cup sweet milk, one half cup molasses. Pinch of salt and a teaspoon baking soda dissolved in milk. Mix the flour, stir in the molasses, then the milk and soda. Steam three hours.

HOME MADE BREAD.

MRS. FRANK GLASS.

Soak a cake of yeast in one quart of water, then add six pints of flour and two teaspoons of salt. Let it stand over night in a rather warm place. In the morning make it up with another pint of water and three pints of flour. Let stand for an hour or so, then knead it well and make into loaves, letting them stand another hour, or until well risen. (Buns made from part of the sponge.) Take a part of the sponge and add two teaspoonfuls of butter and one egg.

TEA BISCUIT.

MRS. HYDE.

One pint of flour (sifted three times,) one teaspoon cream of tartar, one half teaspoon of soda, two teaspoons of sugar, pinch of salt, one dessert spoon of lard or butter, moisten with milk, and yolk of beaten egg.

TAFFY BUNS.

MISS M. W. HOME.

Make a good biscuit crust, roll out rather thin spread with the following mixture. Three quarters of a cup brown sugar, one quarter of a cup of butter mixed together until smooth, roll as you would a roly-poly, cut in slices about an inch thick, and bake in rather a hot oven.

SPANISH BUN.

MRS. THOM.

One and one half cups sugar, four eggs, leave out the whites of three for icing, three quarters of a cup of butter, one cup milk, one tablespoonful cinnamon, one teaspoon ginger, one half nutmeg, two cups flour, three teaspoonfuls baking powder. Bake in flat tin well greased. Icing. Take three whites of three eggs and beat to a stiff froth, then add a cup of light brown sugar, while the cake is hot spread this over, return to the oven and brown.

FRENCH ROLLS OR TWISTS.

MISS LAMPSON.

One quart of milk, one teaspoonful of salt, one small cup brewer's yeast, flour enough to make a stiff batter. Let it rise, and when very light, work in one egg and two spoonfuls of butter, and knead in flour till stiff enough to roll. Let it rise again, and when very light, roll out, cut in round or braids or any shape preferred. N. B. The egg and butter may be omitted.

BUTTER-MILK SCONES.

MRS. FRANK LAURIE.

One quart of flour, two teaspoonfuls cream of tartar and one of baking soda, a little piece of butter the size of an egg and one teaspoonful of salt; mix the butter well in the flour with the hands, put the salt, baking powder into the flour when sifting, add enough butter-milk to thicken. Bake in a moderate oven.

GRAHAM MUFFINS.

MADAME J. T.

One cup Graham flour, one half cup ordinary flour, three quarters cup milk two tablespoons sugar, one large teaspoon baking powder, one large tablespoon butter, one beaten up egg and salt.

MUFFINS.

MRS. GILMOUR.

Butter the size of an egg, one tablespoonful of sugar, one teaspoonful of salt, two mashed potatoes, one and one half cups of tepid water or milk, one cake of yeast, flour enough to make a stiff batter. Put to rise over night, and in the morning put into buttered rings; put to rise again until rings are full, then bake in a slow oven.

MUFFINS.

MRS. HENRY THOMSON.

Two cups sweet milk, four cups of flour, two eggs, two tablespoons of melted butter, four teaspoons baking powder and pinch of salt.

POP OVERS.

MRS. FARQUHARSON SMITH.

A breakfast cup of flour, a cup of milk, three eggs and a pinch of salt: beat the eggs very well, add them to the milk and beat in the flour; the mixture ought to be the consistency of good custard. Butter the moulds very well before putting in the batter; don't put more than a tablespoonful in each. The oven should be very hot and the pop-overs will only take ten minutes to bake.

POP OVERS.

MISS M'GEE.

Three eggs well beaten, add a tablespoon of melted butter and a little salt, pour this mixture over one cup of flour and add milk enough to make a thin batter.

JOHNNY CAKE.

MRS. STUART OLIVER.

One pint of sour milk, one teaspoonful of soda, (good) one egg, butter size of an egg, two tablespoonfuls of sugar, about two small cups each of Indian meal and flour (to make a thin batter.)

SHORT-CAKE.

MRS. R. M. STOCKING.

One pint of flour, one cup of sour cream, one small teaspoon soda, three eggs.

SHORTBREAD.

MRS. W. REID.

Place on a bake-board two pounds of sifted flour, one pound butter (if salt, wash,) and half a pound of sugar; this quantity will make four cakes. Knead all altogether and when well mixed form into cakes half an inch thick, pinch round the edge, and probe all over with a fork, place some confits in the centre, then a sheet of stiff paper under each cake, place on the baking sheet and bake in an oven of moderate heat.

ALMOND SHORTBREAD.

MRS. W. COOK.

One pound ground sweet almonds, eight ounces sugar, eight ounces sifted flour, eight ounces good butter. The yolks of eight eggs, about eight drops of essence of ratafia. First see that the ground almonds are fresh. Mix them with the flour and sugar and then very, very carefully add a few drops of ratafia. Mix everything thoroughly. Make a space in centre, and in this drop the yolks of the eggs. Then melt the butter, add that and mix up the whole together until it is a nice firm stiff paste. This should now be rolled a great many times; cannot be rolled too much. When sufficiently rolled to appear like a strip of cream coloured satin a quarter of an inch thick, cut in small squares with a sharp knife. Pinch the edges of each square and in centre of each cake, put a split half of blanched almond. Butter baking tins and bake in a moderate oven to a fine pale yellow tint. These are delicious and are particularly good in summer eaten with fruit.

SCOTCH SHORT BREAD.

MRS. BLAIR.

One pound of flour, one half pound butter, six ounces sugar; cream butter and sugar, add flour. Roll into a smooth ball and work down until half an inch in thickness, an operation which is rather difficult for a novice, as it is apt to crack at the edges; but the knack is soon learned, and the more it is worked the better. Prick with a small skewer, strew with large carraway comfits, and bake slowly, a pale brown.

BANANA FRITTERS.

MRS. GEORGE ELLIOTT.

Take six bananas, peel and dip in beaten white of egg, then roll in bread crumbs. Fry in butter a golden brown. Put them on a dish, squeeze lemon juice over them, also a little sifted sugar.

APPLE FRITTERS.

MRS. HARRY LAURIE.

Three tart apples, two eggs; one cup milk; one teaspoonful salt; about one and one half cups of flour; one teaspoonful baking powder. Pare and core the apples; cut them into rings; dust with sugar and cinnamon; stand aside to use. Beat eggs without separating until light; add milk, salt and sufficient flour to make a soft batter; beat well and add the baking powder; beat again; Have ready very hot a deep pan of lard, dip each ring of apple in the batter, drop it in the fat and fry until brown. Serve hot, dusted with powdered sugar.

FRENCH PANCAKES.

MRS. BENSON BENNETT.

Four eggs, weight of four eggs in butter, sugar and flour, one half a teaspoonful of soda, one half teaspoonful of cream of tartar. As much milk as will make a batter. Beat the butter and sugar to a cream, add the four eggs well beaten stir in all the other ingredients. Bake in tin plates.

SCOTCH HAGGIS.

MRS. ANDREW T. LOVE.

Boil a sheep's draught for three quarters of an hour in as much water as will cover it. Grate down the liver and mince the heart and lights very fine. Mince two pounds of onions, and two pounds of beef suet, put in three or four handsful of oatmeal with pepper and salt to taste. Having these ingredients very well mixed, put them into the bag with a little of the boilings of the draught. Pick the bag well to prevent its bursting. It requires from three to four hours boiling, so if you make it a day or two before you intend using it, it is better to boil it two hours after it is made, and two hours when going to use it. Great care must be taken in having the bag very particularly scraped and cleansed by frequent washings in salt and water. The liver and heart, etc., are better, to be boiled before, then they can be grated down easily. Half of this receipt makes a very good sized Haggis.

Lector House believes that a society develops through a two-fold approach of continuous learning and adaptation, which is derived from the study of classic literary works spread across the historic timeline of literature records. Therefore, we aim at reviving, repairing and redeveloping all those inaccessible or damaged but historically as well as culturally important literature across subjects so that the future generations may have an opportunity to study and learn from past works to embark upon a journey of creating a better future.

This book is a result of an effort made by Lector House towards making a contribution to the preservation and repair of original ancient works which might hold historical significance to the approach of continuous learning across subjects.

HAPPY READING & LEARNING!

LECTOR HOUSE LLP
E-MAIL: lectorpublishing@gmail.com

9 789353 445768